BOOK 2

Fire on the Water

THE AUTHOR AND THE ILLUSTRATOR

JOE DEVER was born in 1956 at Woodford Bridge in Essex. When he first left college, he became a full-time musician with a large London recording studio. Then on a business trip to Los Angeles in 1977, he discovered a role-playing game called 'Dungeons and Dragons' and was instantly hooked. In 1982 he won the Advanced Dungeons and Dragons Championship in America, where he was the only British competitor. He has since appeared on national TV, radio and in the papers in connection with his hobby.

The Lone Wolf adventures are the culmination of many years of developing the world of Magnamund, and Joe looks forward to revealing more of the wonders of the Lastlands in future books.

Born in 1952, GARY CHALK grew up in rural Hertford-shire. Through an interest in history, he began playing wargames at the age of fifteen – a hobby he still enjoys today. When he first graduated from college with a BA in design, Gary spent three years training in a studio before becoming a teacher in art and design.

He was working as a children's book illustrator when he became involved in adventure gaming, an interest which eventually led to the creation of several successful games including 'Cry Havoc', 'Starship Captain' and 'Battlecars' (co-designed with Ian Livingstone), and on the bestselling 'Talisman' game.

For Titus, Ben Ryan and Victoria

A Sparrow Book
Published by Arrow Books Limited
17–21 Conway Street, London W1P 6JD

An imprint of the Hutchinson Publishing Group

London Melbourne Sydney Auckland
Johannesburg and agencies throughout the world

First published 1984

© Joe Dever and Gary Chalk 1984
Illustrations © Joe Dever and Gary Chalk 1984

This book is sold subject to the condition that it shall
not, by way of trade or otherwise, be lent, resold,
hired out, or otherwise circulated without the
publisher's prior consent in any form of binding or
cover other than that in which it is published and
without a similar condition including this condition
being imposed on the subsequent purchaser.

Set in Linoterm Souvenir Light
by JH Graphics Ltd, Reading, Berks

Printed and bound in Great Britain
by Anchor Brendon Ltd,
Tiptree, Essex

ISBN 0 09 935900 6

LONE WOLF

BOOK 2

Fire on the Water

Written and illustrated
by Joe Dever and Gary Chalk

SPARROW
BOOKS

ACTION CHART

KAI DISCIPLINES NOTES

1	Sixth Sense
2	Tracking
3	Weaponskill in Mace +2 C.S.
4	Mindblast +2 C.S
5	Mindshield
6	Hunting

You can have 6th Discipline if you have completed Book 1 successfully.

WEAPONS (maximum 2 Weapons)

1	Axe Mace +2 C.S.
2	Sword +9

If combat entered holding Weapon and appropriate Weaponskill +2CS.
If combat entered carrying no Weapon —4CS.

BACKPACK (maximum 8 articles)

ITEMS

Map
Healing Potion +4 EP

Can be discarded or changed when
not in combat.

MEALS

~~1~~ ~~3~~ ~~2~~ ~~10~~

—3 EP if no Meal
available when
instructed to eat.

SPECIAL ITEMS

Helmet + 2EP
Crystal Star
Seal of Hammerdal
& Guinspur + 5EP

BELT POUCH
Containing Gold Crowns
(maximum 50)

~~5~~
~~31~~ ~~36~~ ~~30~~ ~~8~~
24 30 ✗

CS = COMBAT SKILL   EP = ENDURANCE POINTS

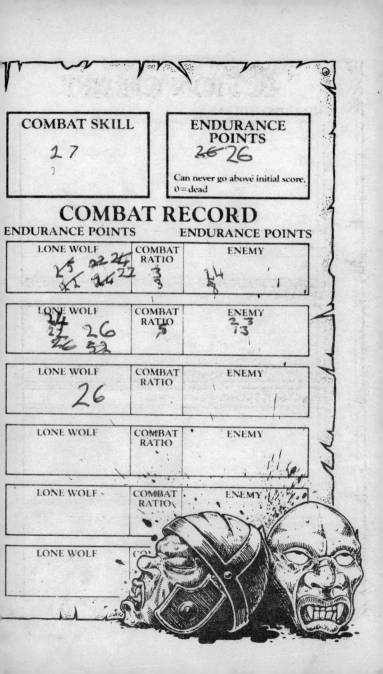

COMBAT SKILL	ENDURANCE POINTS
27	26 26
?	Can never go above initial score. 0 = dead

COMBAT RECORD

ENDURANCE POINTS

ENDURANCE POINTS

LONE WOLF	COMBAT RATIO	ENEMY
25 22 24 22 24 22	3 3	24 1
LONE WOLF 24 27 26 26 32	COMBAT RATIO 5	ENEMY 2 3 13
LONE WOLF 26	COMBAT RATIO	ENEMY
LONE WOLF	COMBAT RATIO	ENEMY
LONE WOLF	COMBAT RATIO	ENEMY
LONE WOLF	CO	

ACTION CHART

KAI DISCIPLINES

NOTES

1	
2	
3	
4	
5	
6	

You can have 6th Discipline if you have completed Book 1 successfully.

WEAPONS (maximum 2 Weapons)

1
2

If combat entered holding Weapon and appropriate Weaponskill + 2CS.
If combat entered carrying no Weapon —4CS.

BACKPACK (maximum 8 articles)

ITEMS	MEALS
	—3 EP if no Meal available when instructed to eat.
Can be discarded or changed when not in combat.	

SPECIAL ITEMS	BELT POUCH Containing Gold Crowns (maximum 50)

CS = COMBAT SKILL   EP = ENDURANCE POINTS

COMBAT SKILL	ENDURANCE POINTS
	Can never go above initial score. 0 = dead

COMBAT RECORD

ENDURANCE POINTS   **ENDURANCE POINTS**

LONE WOLF	COMBAT RATIO	ENEMY
LONE WOLF	COMBAT RATIO	ENEMY
LONE WOLF	COMBAT RATIO	ENEMY
LONE WOLF	COMBAT RATIO	ENEMY
LONE WOLF	COMBAT RATIO	ENEMY
LONE WOLF	CO	

(Spare copy of *Action Chart*)

THE STORY SO FAR . . .

In the northern land of Sommerlund, it has been the custom for many centuries to send the children of the Warrior Lords to the monastery of Kai. There they are taught the skills and disciplines of their noble fathers.

In olden times, during the Age of the Black Moon, the Darklords waged war on Sommerlund. The conflict was a long and bitter trial of strength that ended in victory for the Sommlending at the great battle of Maakengorge. King Ulnar and the allies of Durenor broke the Darklord armies at the pass of Moytura and forced them back into the bottomless abyss of Maakengorge. Vashna, mightiest of the Darklords, was slain upon the sword of King Ulnar, called 'Sommerswerd', the sword of the sun. Since that age, the Darklords have vowed vengeance upon Sommerlund and the House of Ulnar.

You are Lone Wolf, a young Kai initiate who was learning the secret skills of the Kai Lords. Two days ago, your peaceful country was plunged into war when a vast Darklord army suddenly invaded Sommerlund and completely destroyed the Kai monastery. All the Kai Lords were in attendance for the feast of Fehmarn, and all were killed as the monastery was surrounded and destroyed, the walls collapsing in on the assembled company. You, the only Kai Lord to survive the massacre, vowed then to avenge their deaths. You knew your first task had to be to warn the King, for without the Kai Lords to lead her armies, your country, Sommerlund, would be unable to mobilize in time to drive the Darklords back.

Your journey to the capital was perilous indeed. The enemy had overrun much of the country and were marching upon Holmgard, the capital itself. But despite the many dangers, you fought your way through to the capital and delivered your warning to the King's court. There you were greatly praised for your skill and bravery but told your mission was not complete: with the Kai Lords dead, there remained only one power in all of Magnamund that could save your people from the Darklords – the Sommerswerd.

After the defeat of Vashna, the Sommerswerd had been bestowed upon the allies of Durenor as a mark of the trust and allegiance that exists between the two kingdoms. In return, King Alin of Durenor gave Sommerlund a magnificent golden ring bearing the royal arms of Durenor. This ring is known as the Seal of Hammerdal. At that time, King Alin vowed that if ever the shadow of the west should rise again to threaten Sommerlund, Durenor would come to the aid of her ally.

The King has given you the Seal of Hammerdal. Your quest is to travel to Durenor to fetch the Sommerswerd back. But meanwhile the enemy have broken through the outer defences to the capital and are preparing to besiege the city wall. As Captain D'Val of the King's Guard leads you to the Royal Armoury to equip you for your mission, the King's words keep coming back to you:

'Forty days, Lone Wolf. We have strength to stand against them for only forty days.'

THE GAME RULES

Seal of Hammerdal

You keep a record of your adventure on the *Action Chart* that you will find in the front of this book. For further adventuring you can copy out the chart yourself or get it photocopied.

During your training as a Kai Lord you have developed fighting prowess – COMBAT SKILL and physical stamina – ENDURANCE. Before you set off on your adventure you need to measure how effective your training has been. To do this take a pencil and, with your eyes closed, point with the blunt end of it on to the *Random Number Table* on the last page of this book. If you pick *0* it counts as zero.

The first number that you pick from the *Random Number Table* in this way represents your COMBAT SKILL. Add 10 to the number you picked and write the total in the COMBAT SKILL section of your *Action Chart*. (ie, if your pencil fell on the number 4 in the *Random Number Table* you would write in a COMBAT SKILL of 14.) When you fight, your COMBAT SKILL will be pitted against that of your enemy. A high score in this section is therefore very desirable.

The second number that you pick from the *Random Number Table* represents your powers of ENDURANCE.

11

Add 20 to this number and write the total in the ENDURANCE section of your *Action Chart*. (ie, if your pencil fell on the number 6 on the *Random Number Table* you would have 26 ENDURANCE points.)

If you are wounded in combat you will lose ENDURANCE points. If at any time your ENDURANCE points fall to zero, you are dead and the adventure is over. Lost ENDURANCE points can be regained during the course of the adventure, but your number of ENDURANCE points can never go above the number you started with.

If you have successfully completed Book 1 of the Lone Wolf series, you will already have your Combat Skill, Endurance points and Kai Disciplines which you can now carry over with you to Book 2. You may also carry over any Weapons and Special Items that you held at the end of Book 1 and these should be entered on your new Action Chart (you are still limited to two Weapons and eight Backpack items). Through your experiences in Book 1 you have learned new skills, and you may choose one extra Kai Discipline to add to your Action Chart. Now read the section on equipment for Book 2 carefully.

KAI DISCIPLINES

Over the centuries, the Kai monks have mastered the skills of the warrior. These skills are known as the Kai Disciplines, and they are taught to all Kai Lords. You have learnt only *five* of the skills listed below. The choice of which five skills these are, is for you to make. As all of the disciplines will be of use to you at some point on your perilous quest, pick your five with care. The correct use of a discipline at the right time can save your life.

When you have chosen your five disciplines, enter them in the Kai Discipline section of your *Action Chart*.

Camouflage

This discipline enables a Kai Lord to blend in with his surroundings. In the countryside, he can hide undetected among trees and rocks and pass close to an enemy without being seen. In a town or city, it enables him to look and sound like a native of that area, and can help him to find shelter or a safe hiding place.

If you choose this skill, write 'Camouflage' on your *Action Chart*.

Hunting

This skill ensures that a Kai Lord will never starve in the wild. He will always be able to hunt for food for himself except in areas of wasteland and desert. The skill also enables a Kai Lord to be able to move stealthily when stalking his prey.

13

If you choose this skill, write 'Hunting: no need for a Meal when instructed to eat' on your *Action Chart*.

Sixth Sense
This skill may warn a Kai Lord of imminent danger. It may also reveal the true purpose of a stranger or strange object encountered in your adventure.

If you choose this skill, write 'Sixth Sense' on your *Action Chart*.

Tracking
This skill enables a Kai Lord to make the correct choice of a path in the wild, to discover the location of a person or object in a town or city and to read the secrets of footprints or tracks.

If you choose this skill, write 'Tracking' on your *Action Chart*.

Healing
This discipline can be used to restore ENDURANCE points lost in combat. If you possess this skill, you may restore 1 ENDURANCE point to your total for every numbered section of the book you pass through in which you are not involved in combat. (This is only to be used after your ENDURANCE has fallen below its original level.) Remember that your ENDURANCE cannot rise above its original level.

If you choose this skill, write 'Healing: + 1 ENDURANCE point for each section without combat' on your *Action Chart*.

Weaponskill

Upon entering the Kai monastery, each initiate was taught to master one type of weapon. If Weaponskill is to be one of your Kai Disciplines, pick a number in the usual way from the *Random Number Table* on the last page of the book, and then find the corresponding weapon from the list below. This is the weapon in which you have skill. When you enter combat carrying this weapon, you add 2 points to your COMBAT SKILL.

0 = DAGGER

1 = SPEAR

2 = MACE

3 = SHORT SWORD

4 = WARHAMMER

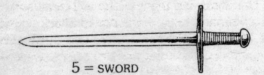

5 = SWORD

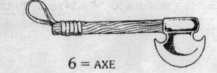

6 = AXE

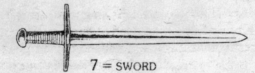

7 = SWORD

8 = QUARTERSTAFF

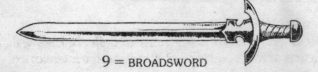

9 = BROADSWORD

The fact that you are skilled with a weapon does not mean that you set out on this adventure carrying it, but you will have opportunities to acquire weapons in the course of your adventure. You cannot carry more than 2 weapons.

If you choose this skill, write 'Weaponskill in ———— + 2 COMBAT SKILL points if this weapon carried' on your *Action Chart*.

Mindshield

The Darklords and many of the evil creatures under their command have the ability to attack you using their Mindforce. The Kai Discipline of Mindshield prevents you from losing any ENDURANCE points when subjected to this form of attack.

If you choose this skill, write 'Mindshield: no points lost when attacked by Mindblast' on your *Action Chart*.

Mindblast

This enables a Kai Lord to attack an enemy using the force of his mind. It can be used at the same time as normal combat weapons and adds two extra points to your COMBAT SKILL. Not all the creatures encountered on this adventure will be harmed by Mindblast. You will be told if a creature is immune.

If you choose this skill, write 'Mindblast: + 2 COMBAT SKILL points' on your *Action Chart*.

Animal Kinship

This skill enables a Kai Lord to communicate with some animals and to be able to guess the intentions of others.

17

If you choose this skill, write 'Animal Kinship' on your *Action Chart*.

Mind Over Matter

Mastery of this discipline enables a Kai Lord to move small objects with his powers of concentration.

If you choose this skill, write 'Mind Over Matter' on your *Action Chart*.

If you successfully complete the mission as set in Book 2 of Lone Wolf, you may add a further Kai Discipline of your choice to your *Action Chart* in Book 3. This additional skill, together with your five or six other skills and any Special Items that you have picked up in Books 1 and 2, may then be used in the next adventure of the Lone Wolf series which is called *The Caverns of Kalte*.

EQUIPMENT

Guard Captain D'Val leads you to the Royal Armoury where your green tunic and Kai cloak are taken from you to be repaired and cleaned. While you await their return, Captain D'Val hands you a pouch of gold for your journey. To find out how much gold is in the pouch, pick a number from the *Random Number Table*. Now add 10 to the number you have picked. The total equals the number of Gold Crowns inside the pouch, and you may now enter this number in the 'Gold Crowns' section of your *Action Chart*. (If you have successfully completed Book 1, you may add this sum to the total of any Crowns you may already possess.)

18

On a large table in the centre of the armoury, a number of items have been laid out for your choice. You may take any two of the following:

SWORD (Weapons)
SHORT SWORD (Weapons)
TWO MEALS (Meals)

CHAINMAIL WAISTCOAT (Special Items). This adds 4 ENDURANCE points to your total.

MACE (Weapons)
HEALING POTION (Backpack Item). This restores 4 ENDURANCE points to your total when swallowed after combat. There is only enough for one dose.

QUARTERSTAFF (Weapons)
SPEAR (Weapons)

SHIELD (Special Items). This adds 2 points to your COMBAT SKILL when used in combat.

BROADSWORD (Weapons)
If you are already carrying Weapons from Book 1, you can take this opportunity to exchange one or both of them.

List the two items that you choose on your *Action Chart*, under the heading given in brackets, and make a note of any effect it may have on your ENDURANCE points or COMBAT SKILL.

How to carry equipment

Now that you have your equipment, the following list shows you how it is carried. You don't need to make notes but you can refer back to this list in the course of your adventure.

1 = SWORD – carried in the hand.
2 = SHORT SWORD – carried in the hand.
3 = FOOD – placed in the Backpack.
4 = CHAINMAIL WAISTCOAT – worn on the body.
5 = MACE – carried in the hand.
6 = HEALING POTION – carried in the Backpack.
7 = QUARTERSTAFF – carried in the hand.
8 = SPEAR – carried in the hand.
9 = SHIELD – slung over shoulder when not in combat otherwise carried in the hand.
0 = BROADSWORD – carried in the hand.

How much can you carry?

Weapons
The maximum number of weapons that you may carry is *two*.

Backpack Items
These must be stored in your Backpack. Because space is limited, you may only keep a maximum of eight articles, including Meals, in your Backpack at any one time.

Special Items
Special Items are not carried in the Backpack. When you discover a Special Item, you will be told how to carry it.

Gold Crowns
These are always carried in the Belt Pouch. It will hold a maximum of fifty Crowns.

Food
Food is carried in your Backpack. Each Meal counts as one item.

Any item that may be of use and can be picked up on your adventure and entered on your *Action Chart* is given capital letters in the text. Unless you are told it is a Special Item, carry it in your Backpack.

How to use your equipment

Weapons
Weapons aid you in combat. If you have the Kai Discipline of Weaponskill and the correct weapon,

you may add 2 points to your COMBAT SKILL. If you enter a combat with no weapons, deduct 4 points from your COMBAT SKILL and fight with your bare hands. If you find a weapon during the adventure, you may pick it up and use it. (Remember you can only carry two weapons at once.)

Backpack Items

During your travels you will discover various useful items which you may wish to keep. (Remember you can only carry eight items in your Backpack at once.) You may exchange or discard them at any point when you are not involved in combat.

Special Items

Each Special Item has a particular purpose or effect. You may be told this when the item is discovered, or it may be revealed to you as the adventure progresses.

Enter on your *Action Chart* a map that you found in the ashes of the monastery.

You begin this section with the Seal of Hammerdal, a ring that you wear on your right hand. Enter it on your *Action Chart* under Special Items.

Gold Crowns

The local currency is the Crown, which is a small gold coin. Gold Crowns can be used on your adventure to pay for transport, food or even as a bribe! Many of the creatures and characters that you will encounter possess Gold Crowns. Whenever you kill a creature, you may take any Gold Crowns that it has and put them in your Belt Pouch.

Food

You will need to eat regularly during your adventure. If you do not have any food when you are instructed to eat a Meal, you will lose 3 ENDURANCE points. If you have chosen the Kai Discipline of Hunting as one of your five skills, you will not need to tick off a Meal when instructed to eat.

Healing Potion

This restores 4 ENDURANCE points to your total when swallowed after combat. There is only enough for one dose. If you discover any other potions during the adventure, you will be told then of their effect. All Healing Potions are Backpack Items.

RULES FOR COMBAT

There will be occasions during your adventure when you have to fight an enemy. The enemy's COMBAT SKILL and ENDURANCE points are given in the text. Lone Wolf's aim in the combat is to kill the enemy by reducing his ENDURANCE points to zero while losing as few ENDURANCE points as possible himself.

At the start of a combat, enter Lone Wolf's and the enemy's ENDURANCE points in the appropriate boxes on the Combat Record section of your *Action Chart*.

The sequence for combat is as follows:

1. Add any extra points gained through your Kai Disciplines to your current COMBAT SKILL total.

2. Subtract the COMBAT SKILL of your enemy from this total. The result is your *Combat Ratio*. Enter it on the *Action Chart*.

Example

Lone Wolf (COMBAT SKILL 15) is ambushed by a Winged Devil (COMBAT SKILL 20). He is not given the opportunity to evade combat, but must stand and fight as the creature swoops down on him. Lone Wolf has the Kai Discipline of Mindblast, to which the Winged Devil is not immune, so he adds 2 points to his COMBAT SKILL giving a total COMBAT SKILL of 17.

He subtracts the Winged Devil's COMBAT SKILL from his own, giving a *Combat Ratio* of −3. (17 − 20 = −3.) −3 is noted on the *Action Chart* as the *Combat Ratio*.

3. When you have your *Combat Ratio*, pick a number from the *Random Number Table*.

4. Turn to the *Combat Results Table* on the inside back cover of the book. Along the top of the chart are shown the *Combat Ratio* numbers. Find the number that is the same as your *Combat Ratio* and cross-reference it with the random number that you have picked (the random numbers appear on the side of the chart). You now have the number of ENDURANCE points lost by both Lone Wolf and his enemy in this round of combat. (*E* represents points lost by the enemy; *LW* represents points lost by Lone Wolf.)

Example

The *Combat Ratio* between Lone Wolf and Winged Devil has been established as −3. If the number taken from the *Random Number Table* is a 6, then the result of the first round of combat is:

Lone Wolf loses 3 ENDURANCE points
Winged Devil loses 6 ENDURANCE points

5. On the *Action Chart*, mark the changes in ENDURANCE points to the participants in the combat.

6. Unless otherwise instructed, or unless you have an option to evade, the next round of combat now starts.

7. Repeat the sequence from Stage 3.

This process of combat continues until the ENDURANCE points of either the enemy or Lone Wolf are reduced to zero, at which point the one with the zero score is declared dead. If Lone Wolf is dead, the adventure is over. If the enemy is dead, Lone Wolf proceeds but with his ENDURANCE points reduced .

A summary of Combat Rules appears on the page after the *Random Number Table*.

Evasion of combat

During your adventure you may be given the chance to evade combat. If you have already engaged in a round of combat and decide to evade, calculate the combat for that round in the usual manner. All points lost by the enemy as a result of that round are ignored, and you make your escape. Only Lone Wolf may lose ENDURANCE points during that round, but then that is the risk of running away! You may only evade if the text of the particular section allows you to do so.

KAI WISDOM

Your mission will be fraught with great danger, for the Darklords and their servants are a cruel and cunning enemy who give and expect no mercy. Use the map at the front of the book to help you steer a correct course for Hammerdal. Make notes as you progress through the story, for they will be of great help in future adventures.

Many things that you find will aid you during your adventure. Some Special Items will be of use in future LONE WOLF adventures and others may be red herrings of no real use at all, so be selective in what you decide to keep.

There are many routes to Hammerdal, but only one will enable you to retrieve the Sommerswerd and return to Sommerlund with the minimum of danger. A wise choice of Kai Disciplines and a great deal of courage should enable any player to complete the mission, no matter how weak his initial COMBAT SKILL or ENDURANCE points score.

The fate of your country hangs on the success of your perilous quest.

Good Luck!

1

Captain D'Val and his guards escort you to the citadel gate where a small covered wagon awaits you. As soon as you clamber in, the gates are thrown open and you are hurried away through the crowded streets of Holmgard. After a short but uncomfortable journey, the wagon stops and the driver pulls open the canvas flap.

'This is the quay, my lord. There is your ship, the *Green Sceptre.*' As he speaks the driver points across the quay to a sleek trade caravel anchored near to the harbour wall.

'The first mate's name is Ronan. You will find him waiting for you across the square at the Good Cheer Inn.' Then the driver bids you farewell and quickly disappears into the teeming crowds.

You reach the inn to find the front doors locked and the window shutters barred. You are trying to decide what to do next when a hand grabs your arm and you are pulled into the darkness.

> If you wish to draw your weapon and attack your unknown assailant, turn to **273**.
> If you wish to try and pull free of his grasp, turn to **160**.

2

You are travelling along a narrow section of coast road which follows a dizzy course beneath high, over-hanging cliffs. A rockfall has blocked the road ahead and you must stop to clear it. You are helping the driver to lever a large rock from the path of the carriage, when you hear the sound of falling rocks. A boulder crashes down from the overhanging cliff, killing the driver before you can make any attempt to save him. He was standing less than six feet away from you at the time of his death.

> If you have the Kai Discipline of Sixth Sense, turn to **42**.
> If you do not have this skill, turn to **168**.

3

You enter a small alleyway behind the shop, at the end of which you can see a horse tethered to a post.

If you wish to take this animal and flee the village, turn to **150**.

If you do not want to take the horse, leave the alleyway by turning to **19**.

4

The tavern is full of brigands and drunks, the good-for-nothing crews of trading ships moored at the jetty, all singing and drinking while some try their strength at arm-wrestling. All are so engrossed that nobody notices you enter. In a far corner, you see the fishermen that robbed you. They are seated at a round table covered with empty ale tankards. You know that if you are to reach Durenor in time, you must retrieve the Seal of Hammerdal and your gold.

If you wish to confront the fishermen, turn to **104**.

If you wish to talk to the innkeeper at the bar, turn to **342**.

If you wish to try and win some Gold Crowns at arm-wrestling, turn to **276**.

5

The door bursts open and in rushes a Helghast, its black sword raised. You strike the creature as it enters the hold and open a terrible gash in its chest. It lets out a hideous cry but although badly wounded, it leaps forward to attack you. You must fight this creature to the death.

Wounded Helghast:
COMBAT SKILL 22   ENDURANCE 20

It is an undead creature. Double all ENDURANCE points that it loses, due to the power of the Sommerswerd. It is immune to Mindblast. If you kill the creature, you may leave via the open hold door.

Turn to **166**.

6

The boy has spotted you following him. Once outside, he turns and runs south. You give chase but he has soon disappeared into the maze of alleyways and warehouses lining the waterfront.

You turn east into Oxyoke Way and walk past another entrance to the trading post. A little further on, you notice a sign above the door of a small shop:

MEKI MAJENOR — ARMOURER & WEAPONSMITH

If you wish to enter the weaponsmithy, turn to **266**.

If you wish to continue walking east, turn to **310**.

7

Dorier jumps away from the table and draws his sword. In an instant, his brother Ganon is by his side. You must fight them both as one enemy.

Dorier/Ganon: COMBAT SKILL 28   ENDURANCE 30

Due to the surprise of your attack, add 2 points to your COMBAT SKILL for the first round of this combat *only*. Because of their combined strength of will, a skill developed during their training as knights, they are immune to Mindblast.

If you win this fight, turn to **33**.

8

Your sleep is deep indeed – and it is a sleep from which you will never awaken. During the night you are bitten by a Sandsnake. Its deadly venom takes only seconds to work.

Your mission and your life end here.

9 – *Illustration I (overleaf)*

It is early morning on the fifteenth day of your quest when you open your eyes to the breathtaking spectacle of Hammerdal, the mountain city. The capital of Durenor, unlike other cities in the Lastlands, does not need man-made fortifications. The encircling peaks of the Hammerdal range offer a far more secure protection to the people within.

The carriage speeds through the lush farmlands surrounding the city with its many towers and wide streets. On a hill in the very centre of Hammerdal stands the King's Tower, a magnificent structure of glass and stone. As the carriage halts at the tower gates, you suddenly realize for the first time that as a wielder of the Sommerswerd, your destiny is to become part of the oldest legend of the Lastlands.

Turn to **196**.

I. The King's Tower, a magnificent structure of glass and stone

10

You pocket the ticket (mark this as a Special Item on your *Action Chart*) and the man takes you to a coach that is waiting near the east gate of the seaport. It is empty and you take a seat near one of its circular windows. You are relieved to find that the seat is quite comfortable, for the journey to Port Bax will take seven days.

Stowing your equipment beneath the seat, you settle back in comfort and doze off.

When you awake, there are five other passengers and the journey to Durenor has already begun.

Pick a number from the *Random Number Table*.

If the number you have picked is 0–3, turn to **51**.
If the number you have picked is 4–6, turn to **195**.
If the number you have picked is 7–9, turn to **339**.

11

Covering yourself with your Kai cloak, you hide inside a large wooden barrel. But it is to no avail, for in less than a minute the trapdoor is thrown open and four angry villagers drop to the stone floor, torches and swords held high in their hands. As you are dragged kicking from the cellar, the screams of the crowd drown your pleas for mercy.

Your life and your quest end here.

12

Captain Kelman unlocks a display case and removes a Samor board. The beautifully carved playing pieces are already in position when he carefully sets it down upon the table.

After somewhat reluctantly agreeing a wager of 10 Gold Crowns, you begin the game.

Pick a number from the *Random Number Table*. If you have the Kai Discipline of Sixth Sense, you may add 2 to this number.

If your total score is now 0–3, turn to **58**.
If your total score is now 4–6, turn to **167**.
If your total score is now 7–11, turn to **329**.

13

Your Kai sense reveals that the left path is the quickest route to Port Bax. You adjust the load of your equipment on your back and set off once more.

Turn to **155**.

14

As the contest begins, you use your Kai Discipline to weaken your opponent's concentration. Beads of sweat stand out on his forehead and his eyes gradually close as he withers under your relentless Mind-blast. In less than a minute he has collapsed to the floor completely unconscious.

Turn to **305**.

15

His look of suspicion changes to one of surprise. 'I believed you to be a trickster, Kai Lord. I must confess that I had planned to teach you a lesson you would not have forgotten in a lifetime. Please forgive my doubts but your story sounded so grave that I refused to believe it for fear it be true. I am sworn to the defence of the border and I cannot leave this tower, but I offer you any of my possessions if they may aid you on your quest.'

He places the following items on a large oak table and invites you to take your choice:

Broadsword
Mace
Quarterstaff
Healing Potion (restores 3 ENDURANCE points)
Enough Food for 3 Meals
Backpack
12 Gold Crowns

As you are about to leave the tower, he points out the direction you should take.

'When you reach the Rymerift, take the track north-wards. You will come to a bridge guarded by the King's men. When they ask for the password, answer them with the word "sunset". The road beyond the Rymerift leads to Port Bax. Godspeed Lone Wolf.'

You thank the brave warrior and leave. You must abandon your horse at the watchtower, for it would be impossible to pass through the dense trees on horseback.

Turn to **244**.

16

You pick up an ale glass and smash it across the edge of the table. The jagged glass is razor sharp. As you draw it across the back of your left hand, a long cut appears trickling blood. Covering this wound with your right hand, you concentrate and feel the warmth of your power as the wound heals. When you remove your right hand, no trace of the cut or any scar remains. The sailor stares at you in amazement.

Turn to **268**.

17

You have pulled yourself halfway through the deck when the door to the hold below bursts open. A Helghast runs shrieking towards you. You cannot escape in time and it badly wounds you in the legs with its black sword. You lose 5 ENDURANCE points and drop to the hold. You must fight this creature to the death.

Helghast: COMBAT SKILL 22   ENDURANCE 30

It is an undead creature, so remember to double all ENDURANCE points that it loses in this combat, as a result of the power of the Sommerswerd. This creature is immune to Mindblast.

If you kill the Helghast, you may leave the hold by the open door. Turn to **166**.

18

The street ahead is completely blocked by wagons which are being unloaded onto a merchant ship. You follow the street as it turns east into Oxyoke Way. To your left is another entrance to the Ragadorn Trading Post. Beyond that, you notice a smaller shop with a sign above the door:

If you wish to enter the trading post, turn to **173**.
If you would rather investigate the weaponsmithy, turn to **266**.
If you wish to continue walking east, turn to **310**.

19

Less than twenty yards away, a small search party is marching along the wet cobblestones. You run towards the darkened doorway of a small shop and quickly enter to avoid the mob. With your heart pounding in your chest, you pray that you have not been spotted.

Turn to **71**.

20

You follow this rat-infested street as it drops steeply to the wharfs and jetties of the River Dorn. From the edge of the waterfront, you see the Ragadorn bridge. It is the only crossing between the east and west sides of this sleazy port. Pushing your way through the crowds of people on the bridge, you enter a rubbish-strewn thoroughfare known as East Trade Lane.

Turn to **186**.

21

The trickster lies dead at your feet. Rolling him over with your foot, you remove several cards from the sleeves of his jacket and throw them on the table. The crowd soon disperses and the tavern is a bustle of noise and activity once more. The other card players retrieve their gold from the table and leave the remainder for you.

To find out how much has been left on the table, pick a number from the *Random Number Table*. (In this instance, 0 = 10 instead of zero.) Now multiply this number by 3. The total is the number of Gold Crowns that are on the table. You may also take the Card Sharp's Dagger if you wish. Remember to mark all the items on your *Action Chart*.

As the body is being dragged outside, you walk to the bar and call for the innkeeper. You press a Gold Crown into his hand and ask for a room for the night.

Turn to **314**.

22

In the morning you are awoken by the cry of the deck watchman: 'Wreckage off the starboard bow!'

Quickly dressing, you climb up on deck and join the captain at the rail.

Pick a number from the *Random Number Table*.

If the number you have picked is 0–4, turn to **119**.
If the number is 5–9, turn to **341**.

23

You chase the furry creature as it hurries along a narrow, twisting passage for nearly ten minutes and are about to give up the chase when the passage opens out into a huge torch-lit cavern. A stunning sight greets your eyes. The cavern houses an entire colony of these strange creatures, all busily sorting through and examining a vast pile of strange objects littering the centre of the hall.

If you have the Kai Discipline of Animal Kinship, turn to **144**.
If you do not have this skill, turn to **295**.

24

It is the crypt of Killean the Overlord. He had been ruler of Ragadorn, but he and many others in Ragadorn died during an outbreak of Red Death plague three years ago.

You suddenly recall a journeyman of your monastery called Swift Fox. He told you tales of his many travels to Ragadorn. The Red Death killed over half the population here. It also killed Swift Fox.

If you wish to return to the tavern, turn to **177**.
If you wish to head west along Tomb Street, turn to **253**.

(contd over)

If you wish to head east along Watchtower Street, turn to **319**.

25

Casting your eye around the crowded tavern, you notice that many of the local villagers are playing various gambling games. Near to the main door, a young rogue has three upturned wooden cups on the table in front of him. He spins them around and challenges anyone to point out the cup that contains a small glass marble. If they guess correctly, he will pay them double the money they have gambled.

If you have the Kai Discipline of Sixth Sense or Mind Over Matter, turn to **116**.
If you do not have either of these skills, turn to **153**.

26 – *Illustration II*

You are staring into the hollow eye sockets of a walking corpse. Twisted and disfigured though he is, you recognize Captain Kelman. You are in fact standing upon the deck of the *Green Sceptre* which sank during the storm twenty-eight days ago, and which has been raised from its murky grave this very morning to join the death-hulk fleet.

The dead captain extends a broken hand towards you and a ghastly voice begs you to lay down the Sommerswerd: 'Put down your sword and my soul will be spared this torment.'

If you wish to place the Sommerswerd upon the deck, turn to **248**.
If you wish to attack the zombie captain, turn to **66**.

II. Twisted and disfigured though he is, you recognize Captain
Kelman

27

You walk for over three hours along the lonely coast road before night begins to fall. You are very tired and you decide to get some sleep and continue at dawn. You remember the tales told by your Kai masters of the wildlands between Sommerlund and Durenor, where packs of wild dogs roam the wastelands at night.

With these stories in mind, you decide to spend the night in the safety of a large leafy tree at the edge of the road.

> Your rest is very refreshing. Restore 2 ENDURANCE points (if any have been lost on your adventure so far), and turn to **312**.

28

The cowardly Szalls squeal in terror and run in all directions to avoid your blows. They have soon fled from the clearing and you turn to help the dying man. He is barely alive and far too weak to talk.

> If you wish carefully to remove the spear from his chest, turn to **106**.
> If you would rather search his pack for useful Items, turn to **320**.

29

You release the lock and slide back the hatch cover. The sudden draught of air causes flames to billow out of the hold. You stumble backwards, clutching your burnt face. Lose 2 ENDURANCE points.

'Fire! Fire!' the cry goes up.

In panic the crew fight to put out the flames. It takes over an hour to control the blaze. The damage is considerable – the entire store of food and fresh water was in that hold, and the fire has completely ruined both, as well as weakened the structure of the ship.

As you stand surveying the wreckage, the captain approaches you, his face blackened by the smoke. He is carrying something in a bundle under his arm. 'We must talk in private, my lord,' he says quietly.

Without replying, you turn and follow him below to his cabin.

Turn to **222**.

30

You land on the rotting timbers and crash straight through to the deck below. You are unharmed by the fall, but the stench of decay that fills your nostrils is overwhelming. You clamber up and unsheathe the Sommerswerd. Four ghastly zombies stagger out of the gloom, their twisted hands extended towards your throat. You must fight them as one enemy.

Zombie Crew: COMBAT SKILL 13   ENDURANCE 16

They are undead creatures, so remember to double all ENDURANCE points that they lose due to the power of the Sommerswerd. They are immune to Mindblast.

If you win the fight, turn to **258**.

31

Your first meeting with the Lord-Lieutenant comes as something of a shock. You had perhaps half expected him to be a servile old man, as are the envoys of the southern lands that plague your King's court with their delegations. The man clad in heavy chainmail standing before you is neither old nor servile. You are soon to learn that Lord-Lieutenant Rhygar is an exceptional man.

Born of a Sommlending father and a Durenese mother, he has become something of a legend in this city. In the last decade, he has led an alliance of the nations to victory against the invading Ice Barbarians of Kalte. Wise in peace, fierce in war, you could not have wished for better company on your quest for the Sommerswerd.

Rhygar orders that a sumptuous meal be served. It is by far the best food you have tasted since the war began. During the feast, you recall the events that have brought you to Port Bax, and reflect on the daunting challenge that still lies before you. After the meal, Rhygar sends for his physician who attends to your wounds. His potions restore 6 ENDURANCE points. Then he advises you to sleep, for you are to leave with the lord-lieutenant for Hammerdal in the morning.

Early next day, you are taken to an enclosed garden at the rear of the consulate where Rhygar and three of his best soldiers await you on horseback. They are to be your bodyguard and guides on the 230 mile ride to Hammerdal. The streets of Port Bax are just beginning to come to life as you ride through the town. Passing under the moss-covered city gate, you now feel confident that your mission will succeed.

Pick a number from the *Random Number Table.*

If the number you have picked is 0–4, turn to **176**.
If it is 5–9, turn to **254**.

32

You awake at dawn to the sound of a shrill cock-crow. You can see the crooked streets of Ragadorn through a veil of heavy rain beating down on the cobblestones outside. It has been six days since you left Holmgard and you are still 200 miles from Port Bax.

You are in the loft of a very large coach station. A group of green-clad men have arrived and have started to clean out one of the coaches. You overhear one of them say that the coach leaves for Port Bax at one o'clock this afternoon and that the journey will take seven days.

You are hungry and must eat a Meal here or lose 3 ENDURANCE points.

(contd over)

After the Meal, if you decide to approach the coachmen and ask to buy a ticket for the journey to Port Bax, turn to **136**.

If you would rather descend the ladder to the street outside, turn to **238**.

33

The other travellers stare with horror and disbelief at what you have done. Before you can explain yourself, there is a loud crash as the front door is thrown open. In rush six armoured soldiers led by the innkeeper. They are the town guard, and the one-eyed innkeeper is screaming at them to arrest you.

If you wish to fight them, turn to **296**.

If you wish to escape by the rear door, turn to **88**.

34

As you close the door of your cabin, you hear the frantic shouts of the crew as they prepare to fight off the attackers. Suddenly you hear the dull thud of something hitting the rear deck followed by the shrieks of creatures you know only too well – Giaks! The Zlanbeast are dropping nets of Giaks on to the ship. The door of your cabin bursts open and you are faced by three of the hideous grey-skinned creatures. Their jagged swords are covered with blood. You cannot evade and you must fight them as one enemy.

Giaks: COMBAT SKILL 16   ENDURANCE 14

If you win the combat, turn to **345**.

35

Stepping over the unconscious soldier, you quickly dash past the tower into the forest. If more guards appear they are likely to attack first and ask questions later.

You have been walking for over two hours when you come to a fork in the road by a stunted oak tree.

If you wish to take the left fork, turn to **155**.
If you wish to take the right fork, turn to **293**.
If you have the Kai Discipline of Tracking, turn to **13**.

36

The food tastes delicious and it is only a matter of minutes before you empty your plate. You decide to take a short nap before meeting the others in the bar room. But as you are about to lie down, a terrible pain grips your stomach. Your legs buckle and you fall trembling to the floor. You feel as if your whole body is on fire. One word repeats itself over and over again in your mind — poison . . . poison . . . poison . . .

If you have some Laumspur, turn to **145**.
If you have the Kai Discipline of Healing, turn to **210**.
If you have neither of the above, turn to **275**.

37 – *Illustration III (overleaf)*

Inside the coach it is warm and dry. Shaking the rain from your Kai cloak, you notice three other passengers on board: two women and a man who is snoring loudly. One of the women looks up and smiles.

'We should reach Ragadorn in six hours,' she says, placing her basket on the floor so that you can sit beside her. You learn that she lives in Ragadorn and she tells you a little about the port.

'Since Killean the Overlord died three years ago, Ragadorn has been ruled by Lachlan, his evil son. He and his mercenaries are nothing but pirates. They bleed the people dry with their heavy taxes, and if anyone complains, they are quietly disposed of. It's a sorry state of affairs. If you take my advice you'll leave Ragadorn as soon as possible.'

During the journey you must eat a Meal or lose 3 ENDURANCE points.

Then in the distance you hear a bell tolling. You look out of the window to see the city wall of Ragadorn. The coach passes through the west gate and pulls to a halt. As you jump to the ground, you are greeted by the awful smell of this dingy seaport. A rusty sign nailed to a wall says 'Welcome to Ragadorn'.

The woman tells you that you can board a coach to Port Bax at the coach station near the east gate of the city.

If you wish to walk north into Westgate Lane, turn to **122**.

If you wish to head south along East Bank Walk, turn to **323**.

If you want to walk east into Axe Lane, turn to **257**.

38

You grab the shaft of the spear and thrust it upwards into the rib-cage of the Helghast. It screams in agony and rage, and releases its grip on your throat. You roll away in time to see the hideous creature fall writhing

III. Inside the coach, it is warm and dry

on the ground, desperately trying to pull the spear from its body.

If you wish to grab the shaft of the spear and drive it deeper into the Helghast, turn to **269**.

If you wish to run away as quickly as possible, turn to **313**.

39

At dusk the coach stops at an inn on the coast road to Port Bax. The cost of a room for the night is 1 Gold Crown for coach passengers and 3 Gold Crowns for anyone else. As you are about to enter, the coach driver demands to see your ticket.

If you have a ticket for the journey to Port Bax, turn to **346**.

If you do not have a ticket, turn to **156**.

40

The muster of the army and the preparation of the Durenese fleet takes fourteen days to complete, during which time you remain as a guest of the king in Hammerdal. As each day passes, you despair for your besieged countrymen of Holmgard and pray that they have enough strength to resist the Darklords until you return.

Every day of your reluctant exile you devote long periods to exercise and meditation. You are also visited by a Durenese herbwarden called Madin Rendalim, who is famous throughout the Lastlands for his knowledge and skill in the healing arts. He restores all the ENDURANCE points you may have lost so far on your adventure, and he gives you a potent Laumspur potion that will restore 5 ENDURANCE points if swallowed after combat. (Mark this under Backpack Items on your *Action Chart*.)

He is also the bearer of some sad news. The body of Lord-Lieutenant Rhygar was found in the forest near to the entrance to Tarnalin. He was killed by Helghast.

If you have the Kai Discipline of Sixth Sense, turn to **97**.

If you do not possess this skill, turn to **242**.

41

You are in luck, for the boat has seen your distress signal and is heading towards you. It is a small fishing boat from the port of Ragadorn. The fishermen are a rough-looking bunch, but they wrap you in a warm blanket and offer you some food. The captain suggests that you sleep, as it will be two or three hours before they arrive back in Ragadorn.

If you wish to take his advice, restore 1 ENDURANCE point and turn to **194**.

If you prefer to stay awake and keep watch for any other survivors of the storm, turn to **251**.

42

You sense that someone is on the cliff above and that you were the intended victim of their attack. Someone is trying to kill you!

Turn to **168**.

43

You swing the Sommerswerd in a wide arc and hit four of the zombies in one sweep, but no sooner do their corpses drop to the deck than others press forward to take their place. You will never kill them all before they overwhelm you. As they start to tear at your cloak, you are forced to dive overboard into the sea to avoid certain death.

Turn to **286**.

44

The venom is in your bloodstream. Your arm feels numb and you are beginning to sweat. The last sound you hear is the gentle lap of the surf and the cries of vultures high above.

Your life and your quest end here.

45

You are galloping along the forest road towards the cloaked riders when you see one of them raise a black staff high above his head. A knot of twisted black steel crowns the tip and it is starting to flow with a vivid blue flame. You are just ready to strike when a searing bolt of energy hurtles from the evil staff and explodes beside you. Thrown sideways by the force of the blast, you tumble into the undergrowth.

Pick a number from the *Random Number Table*.

If the number you have picked is 0–7, turn to **311**.
If it is 8–9, turn to **159**.

46

You try hard to remember the significance of the orange door, but without success.

If you wish to enter this shop, turn to **214**.
If you wish to continue on your way, turn to **230**.

47

The soldiers quickly descend from the roof of the hut and grab their spears. They advance towards you and one of them shouts, 'Password, stranger!'

If you know the correct password for this bridge, turn to **111**.
If you do not, turn to **307**.

48

Pointing at a jug of ale on the bar, you tell the sailor to watch very closely. Closing your eyes, you concentrate on the jug until you can picture it in your mind's eye. As you will the jug to rise in the air, you hear the sailor gasp in amazement.

Turn to **268**.

49

For three days and nights, the fleet of Durenor spread canvas and sail swiftly towards the Holmgulf. But although the voyage is fast, each ship in the fleet is cursed by misfortune. Sails tear, ropes mysteriously untie themselves and timbers warp and leak. The men become short-tempered in the cramped quarters and fighting, often to the death, is common-place. By the third night of the voyage, Lord Axim is close to despair.

'Never have I suffered such a wretched journey. No enemy has been sighted nor battle fought, yet half my men are either ill or wounded, and we have lost two of our finest ships. We have been jinxed by an evil moon. How I pray that it would wane, for even if we were to arrive in Holmgard this very night I fear we are too weak to break the siege.'

As he speaks, you can see the dawn of the next day breaking. You think it may bring promise of relief, but the calm waters that now surround the fleet contain a far deadlier threat.

Turn to **100**.

50

The priest suddenly leans forward and donates another Crown to the plate and the coach is allowed to continue on its way. 'Perhaps you can return the favour sometime in the future, my son,' he says and returns to his seat before you can reply. But you notice how strange it is that the hood of his robe keeps his face in constant shadow.

You are soon across the swollen river and the journey continues.

Turn to **249**.

51

After nearly an hour, the coach stops at the shrine of Kalanane. It is said that this shrine is built upon the grave of King Alin, the first ruler of Durenor, and all around the shrine grow clumps of Laumspur.

If you wish to pick some of this herb, turn to **103**.
If you do not, return to the coach by turning to **249**.

52

Suddenly from out of the darkness above, there is a blood-chilling cry. You look up to see the glowing red eyes of a Helghast as it charges down the steps straight at you. You scream in terror and frantically search for a weapon.

If you have a Magic Spear, turn to **338**.
If you do not, turn to **234**.

53

You hear whispering among the crew and catch the words 'ghost-ships' and 'cursed voyage', but the whispering stops when the captain's voice calls for all hands on deck. A silence descends on the *Green Sceptre* as Captain Kelman addresses the crew in a loud voice.

'Men, we are three days' sail from Port Bax, but with a strong wind and a stout heart we'll drop anchor and feast there in two. The fire has claimed many of our provisions and rations are hereby cut to one meal a day. A guard shall be placed upon the freshwater cask. But we are strong. We shall endure. Any man found thieving will receive a hundred lashes. That is all.' The crew seem unhappy at the captain's decision, but none of them dares to challenge his authority.

Later that afternoon, you are invited by both the crew and by the captain to take your evening meal with them.

If you wish to eat with the captain, turn to **321**.
If you wish to eat with the crew, turn to **154**.

54

As you race through the door, you are knocked off your feet by the force of a spear thrust into your chest. As the moonlight fades, the last thing you see of this world is a circle of screaming villagers as they stab and hack you to death.

Your life and your quest end here.

55

A large man dressed in a leather apron is busily sharpening a fine Broadsword. He is seated at a grindstone that sends a shower of sparks high into the

air every time he touches the blade to it. He bids you good evening and offers you the Broadsword.

'Tis a fine blade, wrought of Durenese steel. It can be yours for only 12 Gold Crowns.'

If you wish to purchase this Broadsword, mark it on your *Action Chart*.

If you leave this shop by the front door, turn to **347**.

If you leave by the rear door, turn to **3**.

56

The innkeeper hands you a key. 'Room 4, second left at the top of the stairs. I expect you out an hour after dawn.'

Your room contains nothing more than a bed, a chair and a small table. You lock the door and prop the chair against it for good measure, before settling down to sleep. You resolve to find some other route to Durenor in the morning.

Turn to **127**.

57

With the back of his gloved hand, the guard knocks the gold from your grasp and it drops into the dark waters of the Rymerift. Pick a number from the *Random Number Table* to determine how much gold you have lost (0 = 10 Gold Crowns).

'We would not sell the security of our land so cheaply,' he says. 'Only a bandit or a fool would try to bribe a soldier of Durenor, and I fancy that you are both.'

Unfortunately, you have insulted their honour and they intend to teach you a harsh lesson.

Turn to **282**.

58

'Bad luck, Lone Wolf. Your strategy is daring, but I think I have you now.'

The captain moves his ornate keystone across the board and you realize that the game is lost. You congratulate him on his mastery of Samor and hand over 10 Gold Crowns.

'Perhaps another game tomorrow evening? Never let it be said that I am not a fair man,' the captain says. 'Perhaps,' you answer cautiously. You bid the smiling captain goodnight before returning to your cabin.

Turn to **197**.

59

You spur your horse towards a cloaked Helghast that is about to strike a helpless soldier. This creature is immune to Mindblast and can only be wounded by a magical weapon.

If you have a Magic Spear, turn to **332**.
If you do not, you must evade the combat and dive into the cover of the forest. Turn to **311**.

60

Halvorc stares in shocked disbelief.

Halvorc: COMBAT SKILL 8   ENDURANCE 11

He is unable to fight back for the first two rounds due

to the surprise of your attack. Do not deduct any ENDURANCE points you may lose during these first two rounds. If he is still alive for the third round of combat, he comes at you with a dagger.

If you win this fight, turn to **76**.

61

Through the pouring rain, you can just make out the dark shape of a city patrol marching towards you. If they should stop you and ask your business in Ragadorn, you could end up in the dungeons of Lachlan the Overlord. Rather than risk being arrested, you retreat along Black Knight Street and quickly turn into Sage Street as the soldiers march past.

Turn to **181**.

62

You enter a large room full of ledgers and files. A man wearing the uniform of a Durenese naval officer is seated opposite at a large desk. He peers at you inquisitively from behind a huge book and says, 'You must have pressing business in the naval quadrant to apply for a red pass at this late hour. I shall need to see your access papers and proof of your commanding officer's authorization.'

If you have collected the necessary documents on
  your quest, turn to **126**.
If you do not have the documents he requires, or
  do not wish to show them to him, you will have
  to risk showing him the Seal of Hammerdal.
  Turn to **263**.

(contd over)

If you do not have either the Seal or the documents, leave the room and return to the outer hall by turning to **318**.

63

You are awoken during the night by the weight of something on your chest. You slowly open your cloak and are horrified to see a sandsnake nestling beneath.

If you want to try to grab this deadly snake behind its head and throw it into the road, turn to **188**.

If you wish to jump up and brush the snake away, turn to **201**.

If you have the Kai Discipline of Animal Kinship, turn to **264**.

64

Ahead you can see a passenger wagon similar in design to those that use the coast roads of Ragadorn. The horses have been cut free and it appears to be deserted. You notice the bodies of three soldiers lying beneath it, their uniforms are heavily bloodstained.

If you wish to search the wagon for food and equipment, turn to **134**.

If you would rather ignore the wagon and continue on your way, turn to **208**.

If you have the Kai Discipline of Sixth Sense, turn to **229**.

65

As you run along Watchtower Street, you hear the curses of the guard fading behind you. You reach Tomb Square, and spot four soldiers marching up Tomb Street towards you. Quickly you head south to avoid them. You have been running along the cobbled street for nearly ten minutes when you spot a large stable and coach station in the gloom ahead. Under cover of the darkness, you enter and spend the night safely hidden in the hay-loft.

Turn to **32**.

66

As you raise the glowing blade, the zombie captain pulls an evil-looking dagger from inside his tattered jacket. You must fight him to the death.

Zombie Captain: COMBAT SKILL 15   ENDURANCE 15

Be sure to remember to double all ENDURANCE points your enemy loses due to the power of the Sommerswerd. The zombie captain is immune to Mindblast.

If you win the combat, turn to **218**.

67

You quickly deduce that the impostor must have escaped by the main entrance to the tavern, and if he is still in the harbour area he must be in or around the main square.

You search the buildings and alleyways round the square but there is no sign of him at all. Rather than waste more time in a fruitless search, you return to the quayside and untie a small coracle from its mooring. As you row towards the *Green Sceptre* you begin to feel uneasy that so early in your mission your enemies seem already to have found you.

Turn to **300**.

68

The guard's expression changes to a sneer of contempt. 'I am a soldier of Durenor. Your gold will not help you here.'

Unfortunately you have insulted his honour and he intends to teach you a harsh lesson.

Turn to **306**.

69 – *Illustration IV*

One of the cloaked strangers removes a black staff from beneath his robes and holds it aloft. A blue flame ignites at the twisted iron tip and a searing blast of energy leaps towards you. There is a deafening crack as the bolt is turned away by Rhygar's shield.

'Give no quarter,' cries the Lord-Lieutenant as he attacks the cloaked staffbearer. His sword slices clean through the robed stranger but he remains unharmed. You suddenly realize why he does not

IV. One of the cloaked strangers holds aloft a black staff and a
blue flame ignites at the twisted iron tip

bleed. He and his sinister companions are Helghast, fell captains of the Darklords. They have the ability to adopt human form but are invulnerable to normal weapons. The Helghast lets out a hideous scream that tears at your mind. Blinded by the sudden pain, you trip and fall into the dense undergrowth of the wooded hillside. Unless you have the Kai Discipline of Mindshield, lose 2 ENDURANCE points from this attack by the Helghast's Mindforce.

Turn to **311**.

70

You gasp with pain as the serpent's fangs sink deeply into your arm. Grabbing the snake behind its ugly head, you rip away the thrashing creature and hurl it into the long grass. But your wound is deep and inflamed by venom.

If you have a Crystal Star Pendant, turn to **219**.
If you do not, turn to **44**.

71

You slam the door shut and draw the bolt. The shop is dark but you can still make out a staircase to your right, a trapdoor in the centre of the floor and another door in the opposite wall. Suddenly there is a crash as an axe splinters a panel of the door behind you. You have been spotted entering the shop and the mob are breaking down the door.

If you decide to open the trapdoor and hide in the cellar, turn to **11**.
If you leave the room by the other door, turn to **54**.
If you decide to run up the stairs, turn to **235**.

72

The innkeeper takes your Gold Crown and places a foaming tankard of ale on the bar. The ale is strong and fortifying. Restore 1 ENDURANCE point to your current total.

If you wish to talk to the innkeeper, turn to **226**.

If you want a room for the night, pay the innkeeper 2 Gold Crowns and turn to **56**.

If you wish to enter an arm-wrestling competition, turn to **276**.

73

The climb is very difficult, for you have only one free hand – the other holds the glowing hilt of the Sommerswerd.

You eventually reach the rim of the tower and quickly hook a leg over the narrow ledge. You are about to jump into the tower and attack when a thin voice makes you freeze.

'How I shall delight in the irony of your death, Lone Wolf.'

The sorcerer is standing in the far corner of the tower,

his left hand pointing at your head. 'Your quest has failed Lone Wolf. Now you must die!'

A blinding flash of orange flame shoots from his hand towards your face.

Turn to **336**.

Placing your hands upon his chest, you try to seal the open wound. He has lost a lot of blood and although he is sweating heavily, his skin is cold to the touch. His eyes suddenly roll open and he shouts a garbled warning.

'Pirates . . . Lakuri pirates . . . beware the red sails . . . repel boarders!'

The captain is soon unconscious once more. You wrap him in blankets and place a cushion beneath his head, but he has drifted off into a sleep from which he will not awake. Back on deck, the bodies of the dead crew have been gathered together. Captain Kelman approaches you and hands you a vicious-looking black scimitar.

'This is no pirate sword, Lone Wolf. This weapon was forged in the furnaces of Helgedad. It is a Darklord blade.'

It is daunting news. If the Darklords have allied the Lakuri pirates to their cause, the voyage to Durenor will be a perilous one. You fling the black sword into the sea and return to the *Green Sceptre*. As you set sail for the east, you watch as the Durenor merchant-man slips beneath the waves.

Turn to **240**.

75

You enter a musty office where two men sit hunched over desks bowed beneath the weight of books and papers.

'Good evening, sir,' says one of the men, his long waxed moustache twitching as he speaks. 'Sir, requires a merchant's pass?'

Before you can reply, the man passes to you a fistful of complicated forms. 'If sir would care to sign these, I can issue sir's pass immediately. The fee is 10 Gold Crowns.'

> If you wish to sign the forms and purchase a white pass, mark it on your *Action Chart* and turn to **142**.
>
> If you do not have enough money or do not wish to purchase the pass, leave this office and return to the hall by turning to **318**.

76

Tearing open his bloodied robes, you are shocked to discover there is no evidence that he was your would-be assassin. All that you find are 2 Gold Crowns and a Dagger. You may take these Items if you wish.

Turn to **33**.

77

During the period of your Kai training, your masters taught you many of the languages and dialects of northern Magnamund, one of which was Szall. The creatures in this clearing are Szalls and they are screaming at you that the wounded man is not a man at all. They say he is a Helghast, a powerful shape-changing servant of the Darklords.

If you believe that they are telling the truth, check what the man has in his pack by turning to **320**.

If you suspect that the Szalls are lying to stop you interfering with their spiteful game, fend them off with your weapon by turning to **28**.

78

You dive backwards, but only just in time to avoid the falling mast as it smashes straight through the deck. You stagger upright and peer into the mass of shattered timbers. Pinned beneath the broken mast is the lifeless body of Captain Kelman.

As you stare in horror, a loud crack fills the air as the storm breaks open the already damaged hull of the *Green Sceptre*. As the ship breaks up you are hurled over the side and into the raging sea.

Gasping for air, you claw your way up to the surface but strike your head on a hatch cover. Lose 1 ENDURANCE point and pull yourself on to this make-shift raft. If you are wearing a Chainmail Waistcoat, you must discard this now or risk drowning. In the grey light of the storm, you watch as the broken ship sinks beneath the heaving sea. You are feeling dizzy and very sick. Hanging on to the cover with all your strength, you gradually slip into unconsciousness.

When you eventually awake, the storm has passed. The only trace of the *Green Sceptre* is the hatch cover on which you lie. By the position of the sun you suppose it to be late afternoon. In the distance, you can see a small fishing boat and beyond it, the coast-line stretches out along the horizon.

If you wish to use your cloak to try to signal to the fishing boat, turn to **278**.

If you want to ignore the boat and paddle towards the shore instead, turn to **337**.

79 – *Illustration V (overleaf)*

The power coursing through your body so over-whelms your senses that you become oblivious to your surroundings. You instinctively raise the blade above your head where a shaft of sunlight suddenly catches upon its very tip and floods the chamber with a blinding white glow. At that moment the true power of the Sommerswerd is revealed to you.

This weapon was forged long before the Sommlending, the Durenese or the Darklords dwelt in the Lastlands. Its makers were of a race that men would now call gods. To release the power that it contains, only a Kai lord may wield it. Should it be used in combat by anyone who is not a Kai lord, its power will fade and be lost forever.

When used in combat, the Sommerswerd will add 8 points to your COMBAT SKILL (10 points if you possess the Kai Discipline of Weaponskill with swords). It has the ability to absorb any magic that is used against its bearer, and it doubles the total of all ENDURANCE points lost by undead enemies, eg Helghasts, in combat. It is the only weapon in all of Magnamund that can kill a Darklord, and for this reason the Dark-lords are bent on thwarting your quest.

You now realize you hold the only power in

Magnamund that can save your people. Slowly the light starts to fade and you become aware of Lord Axim's hand upon your shoulder.

'Come, Lone Wolf, there is much preparation for your return to Sommerlund.'

You sheathe the Sommerswerd in its jewelled scabbard and follow Lord Axim as he leaves the King's chamber.

Make the necessary adjustments to your COMBAT SKILL total now that you possess the Sommerswerd. Note the powers of the sword under the Special Items section of your *Action Chart*.

Turn to **40**.

80

The knight sheathes his broadsword and ushers you inside the tower. You follow him to a large room at the top of a flight of stone steps, where a log fire blazes warmly.

'If you are who you claim to be, you must be in possession of the Seal of Hammerdal. Show it to me,' he orders.

If you wish to show him the Seal, turn to **15**.
If you do not have the Seal, or do not wish to show it, turn to **189**.

81

You awake the following morning to the cries of the lookout from high in the crow's nest above.

'Longboat adrift off the port stern!'

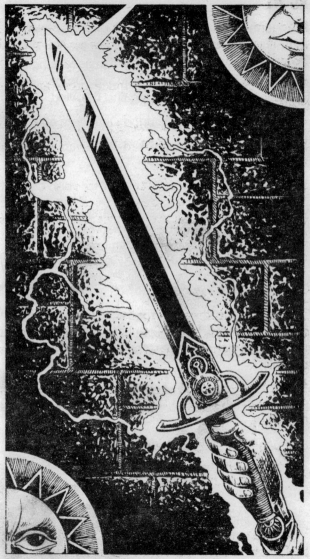

V. At that moment the true power of the Sommerswerd is revealed to you

You climb up on the deck and meet the captain, bracing yourself against the fresh breeze. Less than fifty yards off the port stern, a damaged longboat bobs up and down in the heavy sea. On board are three men huddled together against the wind.

Pick a number from the *Random Number Table*.

If the number you have picked is *0–4*, turn to **260**.
If it is *5–9*, turn to **281**.

82

When you are certain that the angry mob have passed, you jump from the hay-wain and run stealthily along the street, dodging from one shadow to the next. To your left there is a shop with a sign above the door.

There is a light in the window and the door is open.

If you wish to enter this shop, turn to **55**.
If you would rather continue your escape, turn to **347**.

83

At the end of Barnacle Street there is a junction. It is now very dark and you will have to find shelter soon.

If you wish to turn left into Cooper Way, turn to **227**.

If you wish to turn right into Unicorn Street, turn to **297**.

84

Just inside the main door sits a kindly old man with a long beard. He is studying a huge leatherbound book that rests on a lectern before him. He has not noticed you enter the city hall.

If you wish to ask him the way to the consulate of Sommerlund, turn to **211**.

If you wish to leave and try to find your own way there, turn to **191**.

85

Viveka kicks over the table. Her reactions are lightning-fast and you have not gained the advantage of surprise over her. She draws her short sword and attacks you.

Viveka: COMBAT SKILL 24   ENDURANCE 27

If you win the fight, turn to **124**.

86

There are many ships of all sizes and nationalities moored on this side of the harbour. The River Dorn, which divides the city of Ragadorn, is always busy.

You are about to give up your search, when you spot the thieves' fishing boat. There is nobody aboard, but a thorough search of the cabin reveals a Mace and 3 Gold Crowns hidden inside a folded hammock. The hammock bears a label that reads:

NORTH STAR TAVERN — BARNACLE STREET

You take the Mace and Crowns and return to Stonepost Square.

> If you choose to go east along Barnacle Street, turn to **215**.
>
> If you choose to go south along Westbank Wharf, turn to **303**.
>
> If you choose to head north along Booty Walk, turn to **129**.

87

As you raise your weapon and strike at the knight, you realize too late that you have made a dreadful mistake, for he is a champion swordsman and the soldiers are from the elite regiment of King Alin IV's bodyguard. Thinking you are a Helghast, they quickly surround you and cut you to pieces.

Your mission and your life come to a tragic end here in Tarnalin.

88

Although night has fallen, a full moon casts a bright light upon the village. Behind the tavern, you see a small wheelwright's shop with two horses hitched to a hay-cart.

> If you wish to take a horse and escape, turn to **150**.
>
> If you wish to hide in the wheelwright's shop, turn to **71**.
>
> If you have the Kai Discipline of Camouflage, turn to **179**.

89

As you jump, you are spotted by the driver. He quickly stops the coach and turns to confront you, a sword already in his hand.

If you wish to stop and pay him for the ride, turn to **233**.

If you wish to attack him, turn to **212**.

90

Two Szalls and three angry villagers are running up the stairs to attack you. You must fight them one at a time.

Villager 1:	COMBAT SKILL 10	ENDURANCE 16
Szall 1:	COMBAT SKILL 6	ENDURANCE 9
Villager 2:	COMBAT SKILL 11	ENDURANCE 14
Szall 2:	COMBAT SKILL 5	ENDURANCE 8
Villager 3:	COMBAT SKILL 11	ENDURANCE 17

You may evade the fight at any time by jumping through a window. To do so, turn to **132**.

If you win the fight, turn to **274**.

91

The boy is thrown out of the trading post by two black-clad guards. The merchant thanks you and offers you the choice of any two Items of his cargo:

> Quarterstaff
> Blanket
> Enough Food for 2 Meals
> Backpack
> Dagger
> 30 Feet of Rope

Choose any two of the above Items and record them on your *Action Chart*. After thanking the merchant, you leave by a side door.

Turn to **245**.

92

The hideous creature lets out one last cry as it collapses at your feet. As you step back to avoid the putrid smell of its rotting corpse, you see three more Helghast advancing towards you. To remain here would be suicide. You shout a warning to Rhygar as you turn and flee for the safety of the woods.

Turn to **183**.

93

Deduct however many Crowns you wish to give to the beggars from your *Action Chart*. They thank you, but many other beggars have appeared and demand that you give them money as well. You eventually push through the crowd and continue on your way.

Turn to **137**.

94

You urge the captain to investigate the vessel, but he ignores your plea and orders the crew to continue with their duties. As the trading ship disappears from view, you stare at it and wonder why the captain was so reluctant to do anything.

You descend below deck and take care to lock the door of your cabin behind you.

Turn to **240**.

95

You spur your horse through the tangle of trees until you enter a small clearing. Six Szalls are jumping excitedly around the writhing body of a man on the ground. A strangely carved spear is stuck in his chest, and lying dead beside him is the body of a Knight of the White Mountain. The creatures are shrieking at each other and appear to be unconcerned with the man's obvious agony.

If you wish to attack the Szalls, turn to **28**.

If you have the Kai Discipline of Healing, a healing potion or some Laumspur, and you want to try to save the man's life, turn to **239**.

96

Your Kai sense warns you that this place harbours evil. You are standing directly outside the orange door when something strikes you.

Turn to **112**.

97

You have noticed during your rigorous training exercises with the Sommerswerd that your Kai Discipline of Sixth Sense has become more sensitive than ever before: you knew exactly what Madin Rendalim's sad news was long before he actually told you. You may find that your improved Sixth Sense will be an important advantage upon your return to Holmgard.

Turn to **152**.

98

Your Kai sense reveals that there are no tracks in this part of the Durenor forest, but it does tell you the correct direction to Port Bax. However, the forest that lies before you is so dense that you will have to abandon your horse at the watchtower before you can continue.

If you wish to press on towards Port Bax, turn to **244**.

If you want to investigate the watchtower, turn to **115**.

99

The following morning you are woken by the cry of the ship's lookout from high up in the crow's nest.

'Ship ahoy off the port bow!'

You clamber up a narrow ladder and join the captain at the stern. 'Your eyes are younger than mine, see what you can make of her, my lord,' he says, and hands you an ornate telescope.

You can make out the red sails and black flag of a Lakuri pirate warship on the horizon.

Pick a number from the *Random Number Table*.

If the number you have picked is *0–4*, turn to **326**.
If the number is *5–9*, turn to **163**.

100 *– Illustration VI (overleaf)*

A veil of sea fog has rolled across the still ocean from the broken spine of land known as the Kirlundin Isles. Strange dark shapes hide within this mist. They are growing larger, and slowly the distinct outlines of ships become plain.

'Prepare for battle!' The admiral's cry is repeated along the many decks of the Durenese fleet.

'All hands on deck!'

As the black ships approach through the fog, a horrific sight befalls you. They are death-hulks, sunken ships crewed by the living corpses of drowned sailors. They have been summoned to the surface by great wizardry, and they are closing for battle. Suddenly the fog vanishes, and you can now see that the death-hulks bar the entrance to the Holmgulf. In the centre of the line is their sinister flagship. Swiftly it sails towards you, a huge ram protruding from its black prow. As it rips its way through the hull of the *Durenor*, you hear the admiral's last desperate order.

'Abandon ship!'

You are now in the thick of the enemy fleet and the *Durenor* is sinking fast.

If you wish to jump on to the deck of the death-hulk flagship, turn to **30**.

(contd over)

If you wish to dive into the sea and try to swim to another Durenese ship, turn to **267**.

101

As you burst into his cabin, the captain looks up in surprise from his chart table. 'Fire in the hold,' you gasp, breathless from your run.

In an instant, the captain is through the door and ordering the crew to fill buckets with water and gather blankets to smother the fire. By the time you reach the forward hold, the smoke is dense. Suddenly the ship is thrown into a frenzy as flames erupt from the hatch cover. It takes over an hour to contain the blaze and the damage is great. The entire store of food and fresh water was in that hold, and the hull has been badly weakened.

The captain climbs out of the smoking hold and approaches you, his face black with soot. He is carrying something in a bundle under his arm. 'We must talk in private, my lord,' he says quietly. Without replying, you turn and follow him to his cabin.

Turn to **222**.

102

Tarnalin is a wonder to behold. Over a hundred feet in height and width, the tunnel runs to the capital on the far side of the Hammerdal range. Usually it is alive with the traffic of wagons and people to and from Port Bax. But as you enter, you find it deserted except for an overturned fruit cart. The road that disappears into the torchlit tunnel is empty and quiet.

VI.   Their sinister flagship swiftly sails towards you, a huge ram
       protruding from its black prow

As you walk along the paved road, you get an uneasy feeling that perhaps the Helghast have arrived at Tarnalin before you. You have been walking for nearly an hour when the tunnel splits in two.

If you wish to take the left tunnel, turn to **64**.

If you wish to take the right tunnel, turn to **164**.

If you have the Kai Discipline of Tracking, turn to **325**.

103

Laumspur is a delicious herb, much sought after in the Lastlands for its healing properties. You have picked enough for one Meal. Eating this meal will also restore 3 ENDURANCE points to your total. (Remember to add this to your *Action Chart*.) You wrap the herb up, and return to the coach with the other passengers.

Turn to **249**.

104

The fishermen stare at you with open mouths as if they have just seen a corpse return from the dead. Suddenly one of them kicks over the table and they make their escape through the back door of the tavern. In one bound, you leap over the table and pursue them out of the tavern, into the darkness beyond.

If you wish to continue your chase, turn to **231**.

If you decide to let them go, turn to **177**.

105

Unfortunately for you, the rope has been nearly cut in two by a sword blow, and it is likely to snap under your weight.

Pick a number from the *Random Number Table* to see if the rope and your luck holds.

If the number you have picked is 0–4, turn to **286**. It it is 5–9, turn to **120**.

106

The carved spear is made of metal, yet it feels as light as if it were made of wood. You notice the shaft is covered in runes and magic emblems. As you carefully pull it from the man's chest, he gives a long sigh of relief. You are about to examine his wound, when you feel a searing pain shoot through your head. It is so strong and painful that you collapse to the ground. You lose 2 ENDURANCE points.

You are amazed to see the man jump to his feet, and then horrified to see the dreadful change that comes over him. The skin of his face appears to writhe and change colour, growing darker and shrinking as it decays on his skull. His eyes burn with a bright red glow and long fangs protrude from his bottom jaw. You choke with fear as you realize it is a Helghast, a nightmarish agent of the Darklords. It is attacking you with its powerful Mindforce. If you do not have the Kai Discipline of Mindshield, you will lose 2 ENDURANCE points for *every* round of combat that you fight with this creature. Normal weapons cannot harm it and it is immune to Mindblast. You can only wound it in combat with the Magical Spear.

Helghast: COMBAT SKILL 22   ENDURANCE 30

You cannot evade this creature and you must fight it to the death.

If you win the combat, you can keep the Spear. Mark it on your *Action Chart* under the Special Items section as a Magic Spear.'

Continue your adventure by turning to **320**.

107

The captain orders his crew to go alongside. As they board the trader, you are shocked by the sight that awaits you. Dead sailors cover the deck, many pierced by arrows. It seems they must have put up a desperate fight to defend their cargo, but not a trace of it remains in any of the ship's holds. Below deck, you discover the captain in his cabin. He is very badly wounded and near to death.

If you have the Kai Discipline of Healing, turn to **74**.

If you do not possess this skill, turn to **294**.

108

One of the wheels jams in a deep rut and three of the large wooden spokes are shattered. You are forced to stop and replace the wheel before you can continue to Port Bax. You volunteer to help the driver by levering the coach axle with a small tree trunk, so that the spare wheel can be slid into position.

You are pushing down on the stout branch with all your strength, when the horses suddenly rear up and race forward. The trunk springs back and catches you square in the face, knocking you backwards to the ground. You are stunned and you lose 2 ENDURANCE points. The driver is not so lucky. The coach has run over him. As the poor man dies in your arms, his last words are: 'No accident . . . I saw – '

If you have the Kai Discipline of Sixth Sense, turn to **343**.

If you do not possess this skill, turn to **168**.

109

Blinking the foul water from your eyes, you can see that the flagship of the death-hulk fleet is now ablaze. Black smoke is pouring from the decks, and tongues of orange and yellow flame flicker from its rotten black hull.

Suddenly, you are aware of the beating of wings directly above you. You are shocked to see a Kraan hovering above, trying to grab at you with its sharp claws. Its hooked talons catch your cloak and suddenly you are snatched up into the air. But it is to be a short flight. You draw the Sommerswerd and sink it into the soft belly of the creature. With a shriek of agony, it releases its grip and you fall. You pray that luck will be on your side and that you will land safely.

Turn to **120**.

110

The guard does not believe you, and he attacks you with his sword.

Watchtower Guard:

COMBAT SKILL 15   ENDURANCE 22

If you do not have a weapon, deduct 4 points from your COMBAT SKILL for the duration of this combat.

You may evade the fight at any time by turning to **65**.

If you win the combat, turn to **331**.

111

The guards reluctantly lower their weapons and allow you to cross the bridge. As you slip past, they stare at you and whisper to each other. Once you are safely across the Rymerift, you quickly hurry on your way in case they change their minds and arrest you. After nearly an hour of walking along the forest road, you arrive at a junction where a signpost points to the east.

PORT BAX – 3 MILES

You smile and set off eastwards. You should be there in just under an hour.

Turn to **265**.

112

You suddenly remember what he said about the shop with the orange door. It is the headquarters of the Silent Brotherhood, Lachlan's notorious secret police. To enter here would be more perilous than entering a roomful of Drakkarim!

You quickly turn away from the orange door and hurry northwards.

Turn to **230**.

113

He is Vonotar the Traitor, renegade wizard from the magician's guild of Toran. He is a master of the black arts and now possesses great power which the Darklords themselves have given him. It was his agents who tried to assassinate you during your quest, and it is he who commands the death-hulk fleet. Destroy Vonotar and you will destroy the evil force that gives power to the death-hulks and their crews.

You may climb the tower and attack Vonotar by turning to **73**.

If you do not wish to risk your life against this powerful magician, escape from this ship by jumping overboard, and turning to **267**.

114

You have walked for over three hours along this lonely coast road when night starts to fall. The land is flat and barren, and you have seen no sign of life here at all. You finally decide to rest beneath the branches of a large tree standing close to the highway. Making a pillow of your backpack, you pull your warm Kai cloak around yourself and drift off into a deep sleep.

Pick a number from the *Random Number Table*.

If the number you have picked is *0–3*, turn to **206**.
If the number is *4–7*, turn to **63**.
If the number is *8–9*, turn to **8**.

115

The area around the watchtower door has been cleared of foliage, and the ground is well-trodden. You are looking for a lock or keyhole in the iron-clad door when it suddenly opens. Standing before you is a Knight of the White Mountain, a broadsword held in front of his face.

'State your purpose and mark your words well. My steel will be my answer if you lie!'

> If you wish to tell this knight the true purpose of your mission to Durenor, turn to **80**.
>
> If you want to lie about why you are here, turn to **324**.
>
> If you want to draw your weapon and attack the knight, turn to **162**.

116

Using your Kai Discipline, you can tell which cup hides the marble, for to you, the clay is as transparent as glass itself.

Pick a number from the *Random Number Table* and add 5 to it. This equals the number of Gold Crowns that you win before the rogue suspects something is wrong and ends the game.

With gold in your purse once more, you return to the bar and hand over 1 Gold Crown for a room.

> Turn to **314**.

117

It is a large passenger wagon similar to those used by highway travellers of Sommerlund. The driver pulls the horses to a halt and stares at you from under the wide brim of his hat. You ask where he's bound for.

'We're bound for Ragadorn – due there by noon today. A seat will cost you 3 Gold Crowns, but you can ride on the roof for only one.'

If you wish to ride inside, pay the driver 3 Gold Crowns and turn to **37**.

If you would prefer to ride on the roof, pay him 1 Gold Crown and turn to **148**.

If you cannot pay the fare, you must let the coach continue and begin your journey on foot. Turn to **292**.

118 – *Illustration VII (overleaf)*

You bid Rhygar farewell and enter Tarnalin. Over a hundred feet in height and width, the tunnel runs to the capital on the far side of the Hammerdal range, and is lit by torches for its entire length. The highway through the mountain is usually alive with the traffic of merchants to and from Port Bax, yet now the entrance and interior are deserted except for an over-turned fruit wagon. As you walk deeper into Tarnalin, a doubt nags at you. Have the Helghast arrived here first?

You have been walking for half an hour when you see a strange creature on top of a wagon in the road ahead. It is two feet high and resembles an overgrown marsh rat. You assume it is some sort of tunnel-dwelling rodent until you notice that it is wearing a splendid jacket of patched leather and carrying what appears to be a spear. As you get nearer, it suddenly turns to face you. Its whiskered nose is sniffing the air and its bright black eyes are peering into the gloom. It sees you and scampers off into the darkness of a smaller tunnel to your left.

If you wish to follow this creature, turn to **23**.

If you wish to ignore it and continue on your way, turn to **340**.

If you have the Kai Discipline of Animal Kinship, turn to **279**.

119

Shattered beams, pieces of planking and torn sails litter the white-flecked waves. It is all that remains of a merchant ship. But then suddenly you notice a body clinging to a broken hatch cover. A rope ladder is quickly lowered and the poor man is brought aboard.

'Pirates!' is all he says before collapsing to the deck. The man is wrapped in a large blanket and taken below. He has suffered many wounds and is close to death.

'This crime bears the mark of the Lakuri pirates,' the captain confides in you, 'but it is unusual to run across them in these waters. They must be in search of a rich cargo to sail so far from their tropical islands.'

As the ship resumes its course for Durenor, you cannot help but wonder if that 'rich cargo' is you.

Turn to **240**.

120

Luck is with you, for you land safely on the deck of the *Kalkarm*, a Durenese warship. The soldiers here have been involved in a desperate battle but have fought off the enemy and are cutting the grappling

VII.   The strange creature is wearing a splendid jacket of patched
leather and carrying what appears to be a spear

ropes that hold the ship to a death-hulk. From out of the smoke strides Lord Axim, his face bloodied and his shield badly scarred.

'Thank the gods you are alive, Lone Wolf. The fight has been bitter and our losses are high, but I am heartened indeed to see you standing before me now,' he says and leads you to the ship's rail. 'Look yonder, their flagship is ablaze.'

Through the fog of war you can see that the huge death-hulk is slowly sinking beneath a plume of dense black smoke. The *Kalkarm* is eventually freed and slowly it manoeuvres out of the tangle of wreckage. A wind begins to stir, filling its tattered sails and carrying away the smoke of battle. Lord Axim orders the Royal Arms of Durenor to be hoist aloft so that other ships can rally to the *Kalkarm*. For the first time since the battle began, you can now see the other Durenese ships. It is an amazing sight, for as the enemy flagship sinks beneath the waves, so every death-hulk on the horizon returns to its watery grave.

'Their sorcery is broken. We have won this battle,' says Lord Axim. And within a few minutes, not one of the death-hulks remains afloat.

Turn to **225**.

121

As you run along Lookout Street, you quickly reach the waterfront where the River Dorn separates the east and west sides of the city. To your left is the Ragadorn Bridge, an ugly construction of rusted iron that provides the only connection between the two halves of Ragadorn. With the shouts of the street thieves echoing in your ears, you push your way through the people crowding the bridge. By the time you have got across, the street thieves have given up the chase, and you enter a rubbish-strewn thorough-fare known as East Trade Lane.

Turn to **186**.

122

This street follows the city wall northwards. On your right you notice a shop with a bright orange door. Unlike all of the other shops in this street, it bears no sign above it. You suddenly remember the tales of a Kai lord who returned from a visit to Ragadorn about a year ago. He mentioned this orange door in one of his many stories.

Pick a number from the *Random Number Table*.

If the number you have picked is *0–4*, turn to **46**.
If the number is *5–9*, turn to **112**.
If you have the Kai Discipline of Sixth Sense, turn to **96**.

123

A strange power is coursing through your body. Instinctively you raise the blade above your head and a shaft of sunlight suddenly catches the edge of the sword and floods the King's chamber with a blinding white glow.

But almost immediately the light starts to fade and you are aware of Lord Axim's hand upon your shoulder. 'Come, Lone Wolf. There is much to prepare for your return to Sommerlund.'

You sheathe the Sommerswerd in its jewelled scabbard and follow Lord Axim as he turns and leaves the king's chamber.

Turn to **40**.

124

You quickly search her body but find no evidence that she was your would-be assassin. You discover 42 Gold Crowns, a Short Sword and a Dagger. Take any of these items if you wish, and mark them on your *Action Chart*.

Turn to **33**.

125

You quickly dash through the side door of the tavern and run the length of the alleyway towards the main square. Through the crowds of people you can see many boats and coracles tied up to the quayside. The thugs are close behind and you must act quickly.

Untying one of the small boats, you jump from the harbour wall and land with a crash, splintering the wooden seat. It has one paddle which you use to make your way towards the *Green Sceptre*, anchored three hundred yards across the water.

Turn to **300**.

126

The man pulls a hidden bell-rope, and suddenly four armed guards burst into the room.

'These documents are forgeries. No doubt you are a spy, or worse perhaps? No matter, you'll soon find out how we deal with criminals in Port Bax. Take him away.'

Before you can explain, you are seized by both arms and marched away to the city jail. All your equipment is confiscated, including all Special Items and Weapons, and you are thrown into a cell full of evil-looking villains. You notice that several of these ruffians bear the strange tattoo of a serpent on their left wrist: the sign of Vonatar the Traitor. By the time the guards have examined your possessions and realized your true identity, you have been strangled to death by the wizard's evil agents.

Your life and your quest come to a tragic end here in Port Bax.

127

You awake at dawn to the sound of heavy rain falling on the cobbled streets outside.

It has been six days since you left Holmgard, and you must eat a Meal here or lose 3 ENDURANCE points. You gather your equipment and leave the room. As you descend the rickety stairs, you see the innkeeper cleaning the floor with a mop and bucket.

If you wish to ask the innkeeper how you can get to Durenor, turn to **217**.

If you wish to leave the inn without speaking to him, turn to **143**.

128

A golden glow runs the length of the Sommerswerd as you raise it high above your head, ready to face your enemy. You are confronted by six grisly zombies and you must fight them as one enemy.

Zombie Crew: COMBAT SKILL 13   ENDURANCE 19

They are undead creatures, so remember to double all ENDURANCE points they lose as a result of the power of the Sommerswerd.

If you win, turn to **237**.

129

You pass several narrow warehouses lining the waterfront, and reach the harbour wall. Here the road bears sharply to the right into Tomb Street.

Marching along the centre of this street are four heavily armed city guards. Rather than be stopped and possibly arrested by these soldiers, you dodge into an alleyway off to your right. The guards suddenly halt opposite the alley entrance. If one of them should turn his head, you will be spotted for sure. Behind you is a small window, leading into a crowded tavern.

Without a second's hesitation, you climb through the window as quickly as possible.

Turn to **4**.

130

The priest approaches you and says, 'You need to rest, as we all do. I understand your problem my friend. Please allow me to practice what I humbly preach,' and with these words he leads you to the bar and places a Gold Crown into the hand of the inn-keeper. 'A room for my friend,' he says and smiles.

Turn to **314**.

131

You ask them what they want of you. In answer, they simultaneously produce long, curved daggers from inside their jackets. Their leader steps forward and demands your gold. As you hesitate, he shouts, 'Take 'im!' and all three attack you.

If you have no Weapon, deduct 4 points from your COMBAT SKILL and fight them bare handed. You must fight them one at a time.

Street Thief Leader: COMBAT SKILL 15 ENDURANCE 23
Street Thief 1:   COMBAT SKILL 13 ENDURANCE 21
Street Thief 2:   COMBAT SKILL 13 ENDURANCE 20

You may evade them during the combat by turning to **121**.

If you kill all three thieves, turn to **301**.

132

You crash to the muddy street in a shower of broken glass. You are winded by the fall, but otherwise unharmed. An angry villager armed with a cudgel tries to smash your skull, but you roll aside, jump to your feet and sprint away down the twisting street before he has struck his blow. Then an ugly Szall on horseback charges towards you with a raised spear. He is about to stab you when you sidestep and grab the weapon, pulling it and the Szall from the saddle.

If you wish to stab the Szall with his own spear, turn to **317**.

If you wish to mount his horse and escape, turn to **150**.

If you wish to keep the Spear, remember to mark it on your *Action Chart*.

133

Looking directly into the sailor's eyes, you concentrate your Mindblast at his open hand. Suddenly the man falls backwards from his chair, clutching his hand as if he had just picked up a red-hot coal. When you explain what has happened to him, he looks at you in amazement.

Turn to **268**.

134 – *Illustration VIII*

Suddenly from out of the darkness there is a blood-chilling cry. You find yourself staring into the glowing eyes of a Helghast. As it tries to close its fingers around your throat, you scream in terror and fall to the ground. The hideous creature tears at your tunic, rending the cloth with its black claws.

If you have a Magic Spear, turn to **38**.

If you do not, turn to **304**.

135

The knight points to the woods behind you and says in a gruff voice, 'There is your shelter.'

VIII.   You find yourself staring into the glowing eyes of a
Helghast

Before you can reply, he has stepped back into the tower and bolted the heavy door. The forest here is very dense and the undergrowth is a tangle of weeds and briars. It will prove impossible to enter the wood on horseback, so you must abandon your mount before continuing on foot.

Turn to **244**.

136

'The fare to Port Bax is 20 Gold Crowns,' says the coachman in a gruff Ragadornian accent.

If you have 20 Gold Crowns and wish to purchase a ticket, turn to **10**.

If you do not have enough money for the fare, turn to **238**.

137

You reach a junction where Beggar Lane turns south into Black Knight Street. A few yards along there is another lane called Anchor Street, which heads off towards the east. The rain has become much heavier now.

If you wish to head south along Black Knight Street, turn to **259**.

If you wish to head east along Anchor Street, turn to **20**.

138

You have been walking for nearly two hours when you reach the peak of a hill and see the Durenor forest stretched out before you. The road bears eastwards and enters the trees at a point where a large wooden tower has been built. You can see the silhouette of a soldier on guard.

If you wish to continue on your journey towards the watchtower, turn to **232**.

If you would rather avoid the guard, make a wide detour and enter the forest further south by turning to **244**.

139

The training that you received in the art of Hunting has taught you to recognize most of the poisonous and non-poisonous fruits to be found in northern Magnamund. These purple fruits are Larnuma, a sweet and nutritious food. You quickly eat your fill and then store enough of them in your Backpack for 2 Meals.

Beyond the Larnuma trees, you notice a wide coast road that disappears towards the east and the west.

If you wish to head east, turn to **27**.
If you wish to head west, turn to **114**.

140

Both guards stare at the Seal in awe. The legend of the Seal of Hammerdal is well-known to all the people of Durenor. It is said that of all the lost treasures of Durenor, the Seal of Hammerdal is the one they would not wish returned. The anxious faces of the two guards show they clearly realize its significance.

One of the guards escorts you across the Rymerift and along a forest road that eventually ends at a junction. A signpost points to the east.

PORT BAX — 3 MILES

'I must leave you now and return to the Rymerift. I fear that war will soon cast its black shadow upon this land and I shall be needed at the border. Godspeed to you Sommlending, godspeed.'

You watch for a few minutes as the soldier returns along the forest track before you set off eastwards. You should arrive in Port Bax within the hour.

Turn to **265**.

141

As the mast smashes into the deck, a splintered beam hits your head and you are knocked overboard. Gasping for air, you fight your way to the surface and catch hold of a hatch cover. You are half-stunned. You lose 2 ENDURANCE points.

You pull yourself on to this makeshift raft and cling to it with all your strength. If you are wearing a Chain-mail Waistcoat, you must discard it now or otherwise you will be drowned for sure.

You feel dizzy and sick. As the heaving sea buffets you relentlessly, you gradually slip into unconsciousness. When you awake many hours later, the storm has passed. By the position of the sun, you judge it to be late afternoon. In the distance you can see a small fishing boat and beyond it, on the horizon, land. The only trace of the *Green Sceptre* is the hatch cover on which you now sit.

If you wish to use your cloak to try to signal to the fishing boat, turn to **278**.

If you wish to ignore the boat and paddle towards the shore, turn to **337**.

142

The man takes your money and hands you a white pass that is valid for the next seven days. You thank him and leave the building. Outside you turn left and walk towards the guards at the end of the street.

Turn to **246**.

143

You head south and follow the quayside until you come to a junction where the street heads off towards the east. Most of the shops in this street are still closed except for one to your right. There is a sign above the door.

JINELDA KOOP – ALCHEMIST
Magical Potions Bought and Sold

If you wish to enter the shop, turn to **289**.

If you wish to continue on your way, turn to **186**.

144 – *Illustration IX (overleaf)*

A large Noodnic, wearing a brightly coloured cloak of patchwork silks, orders several of his people to arm themselves and drive you out of the hall. When you speak to them in their own language, a hush of astonishment fills the cavern. Never before have they encountered a human being who could actually speak their tongue. For some of them it is too much to grasp, and they stare at you open-mouthed, their furry little arms hanging loosely by their sides.

Then the large Noodnic addresses you, saying he is the leader of this colony. His name is Gashgiss and he welcomes you and invites you to join him on top of a raised platform in the centre of the chamber.

'Yooze notta Dureneeze man-man, eh? Whereza yooze come za from, eh?' questions Gashgiss, in his strange Noodnic accent.

You tell him that you are a Sommlending on your way to Hammerdal. He looks at you nervously, then asks, 'Yooze notta Blackscreamerz, eh?' You realize that the 'Blackscreamerz' that Gashgiss refers to are Helghast. You learn that two of them arrived in Tarnalin over two hours ago, and caused quite a panic in the main tunnel. Gashgiss knows where they are lying in ambush, waiting for you to appear.

'Iza show yooze z'way past zem, eh?' he offers. You nod your agreement and follow him down the steps of the platform, to the hall below.

The Noodnics seem to have overcome their shock and react to you now as if you were one of them. Before you leave, a pretty female Noodnic offers you some food for your journey ahead. There is enough for two Meals. You thank her for her generosity and then follow Gashgiss along one of the many passages leading out of the cavern. After an hour of trekking through the dark, he stops and points towards a shaft of light that is pouring through a crevice in the far distance. 'Yooze goez left, yooze be zafe,' he says.

IX.   The large Noodnic,   wearing a brightly coloured cloak of
        patchwork silks, addresses you

You thank Gashgiss for his help and silently thank your Kai masters who taught you the skill of Animal Kinship. The many years of instruction have probably saved your life. You squeeze through a fissure in the rock wall and drop three feet to the pathway below. You are thinking how kind the Noodnics were when you discover that they have stolen all your gold! You will have to mark this on your *Action Chart*.

Continue along the tunnel and turn to **349**.

145

You are becoming weaker and weaker. After what seems an eternity of painful struggle you find the Laumspur and force yourself to swallow the dry leaves. Within seconds you are violently sick, after which you drift off into a restless sleep.

It is nearly an hour before you awake and you still feel dreadfully ill. Deduct 5 ENDURANCE points.

As you slowly regain your strength, the shock of what has happened soon turns to anger. You grab your equipment and stagger out of the room, intent on confronting your would-be assassin.

Turn to **200**.

146

You were right. The cloud is made of huge Zlanbeast and many Kraan, a smaller species but one that is just as deadly. Hanging below their black bellies are nets full of Giaks. As the Zlanbeast descend on the *Green*

Sceptre, a net of shrieking Giaks crashes on to the deck behind you. Some are crushed in the fall, but many more have survived and waste no time attacking you. You must fight them as one enemy.

Giaks: COMBAT SKILL 15   ENDURANCE 15

If you win this combat, turn to **345**.

147

Your senses reveal that the path is a dead end. The only way that you can cross the Rymerift and reach Port Bax is via the bridge.

Turn to **47**.

148

You wrap yourself in your Kai cloak and raise the hood. The driver shouts and whips the horses and soon you are on your way along the tree-lined coast road to Ragadorn. During the journey, you talk to the driver and learn some useful things about the seaport of Ragadorn.

Ever since Killean the Overlord died three years ago, Ragadorn has been ruled (or misruled according to the driver) by his son, Lachlan. It seems that he and his men are nothing more than pirates. They tax the people heavily, and murder all who oppose them.

You are hungry and during the coach ride, you must eat a Meal or lose 3 ENDURANCE points.

At last, in the distance, you can just make out the city wall of Ragadorn. A bell is tolling – it rings twelve times. Eventually the coach passes through the west gate of the wall and pulls to a halt.

'If you want to get to Durenor, you can catch a coach from the stable at the east gate. Best hurry mind, it leaves at one o'clock,' the driver tells you.

You thank the driver for the advice and jump to the cobblestones below. For the first time, you suddenly notice the awful smell of this dirty seaport. A rusty sign nailed to a rot-infested house says 'Welcome to Ragadorn'.

> If you wish to go south along Westgate Lane, turn to **323**.
> If you wish to head north along East Bank Walk, turn to **122**.
> If you wish to head east into Axe Lane, turn to **257**.

149

You can sense that this guard is a loyal Durenese soldier. If you were to attempt to bribe him, he would be likely to consider it a grave insult and attack you.

> If you wish to show him the Seal of Hammerdal, turn to **223**.

If you would prefer not to show it, if you do not have it, or if you wish to pretend to be a merchant on your way to Port Bax, turn to **250**.

150

You spur the horse along the twisting village street, across a wooden bridge and up a steep path towards the crest of the cove. In the light of the moon, you catch a glimpse of a signpost pointing eastwards.

You ride all night without sleep. As the dawn breaks, you are greeted by a startling change of landscape. The barren Wildlands have given way to moors and waterlogged fens. And a dark shadow runs the length of the eastern horizon for as far as the eye can see. This is the Durenor forest, the natural frontier of the mountain kingdom where it borders the untamed Wildlands. It is indeed a welcome sight.

You are no more than a day's ride from Port Bax, but you are tired after your night ride and you must eat a Meal or lose 3 ENDURANCE points. If you have the Kai Discipline of Hunting, you may use this skill to trap a wild moor-rat or marshbird for your breakfast.

After an hour's ride you come to a fork in the road. There is no signpost.

If you wish to take the left fork, turn to **261**.
If you wish to take the right fork, turn to **334**.

151

Using your skill to mimic the gruff Ragadornian accent, you bluff the guard, saying that there is a fight in Tomb Square. You say that the city watch have been overpowered, and that he is needed at once.

To see if your bluff has been succesful, pick a number from the *Random Number Table*.

If the number you have chosen is *0–4*, turn to **262**.
If it is *5–9*, turn to **110**.

152

It is early in the morning of the thirty-third day of your quest, when you ride into Port Bax with Lord Axim at your side.

The preparations for war have been completed. The galleons of the Durenese warfleet lie at anchor in the harbour, impatiently awaiting the order to set sail for Sommerlund. On board each ship are many brave soldiers from the mountain kingdom, a tough army of skilled warriors, eager to face the Darklords in battle. Each man has sworn to avenge their besieged allies, or die in the attempt.

You are to sail back to Holmgard aboard the flagship *Durenor*, a warship whose great curving prow and tall masts emphasize its sheer power and strength. You and Lord Axim are taken aboard and welcomed by

Admiral Calfen, commander of the fleet, and then the fleet prepares to set sail.

In less than an hour, the harbour lies far behind you. The domes of Port Bax are now merely dots on the horizon.

Pick a number from the *Random Number Table*.

If the number you have picked is *0–3*, turn to **216**.
If the number is *4–6*, turn to **49**.
If the number is *7–9*, turn to **193**.

153

You forget about the rogue with his cup and marble game and instead watch a card game in progress near the tavern stairs. You notice that one of the players is cheating.

If you wish to challenge the man, turn to **241**.
If you would rather ignore what you have seen, turn to **130**.

154

The crew's quarters are cramped and stifling. But despite a lack of space and a poor evening meal (so poor in fact, that you lose 2 ENDURANCE points!) the men are pleased that their invitation was accepted and you are treated as an honoured guest.

After supper, they invite you to play 'Portholes' with them, and wager a little gold on the fall of the dice.

If you wish to try your luck, turn to **308**.
If you would prefer to decline the offer, bid them goodnight and return to your cabin by turning to **197**.

155

After travelling a mile along the left track, you arrive at a long stone bridge. At first glance, the river that it crosses seems to be swollen and in danger of flooding the banks. Then you realize that this is the Rymerift. The waters of the Rymerift are two miles across at the widest point and over a mile deep for most of its length. Here, the land has slipped away and a natural gap has appeared separating Durenor from the rest of Magnamund.

There is a signpost at the entrance to the stone bridge.

PORT BAX – 3 MILES

You breathe a sigh of relief, for you are on the correct path and should be in the city within the hour.

Turn to **265**.

156

The driver becomes very angry and shouts, 'There's a long walk ahead of you, stranger,' as he slams the door in your face. You cannot afford to buy a room for the night, so you decide to bed down with the horses in the stable next door.

Turn to **213**.

157

The guard is furious and charges down the stairs at you, his sword raised above his head. If you do not have a weapon, remember to deduct 4 points from your COMBAT SKILL and fight the guard open-handed.

Watchtower Guard:
COMBAT SKILL 15   ENDURANCE 22

You may evade this combat at any time by turning to **65**.

If you win the combat, turn to **331**.

158

The priest does not seem to be surprised by your attack, and he draws a black sword from beneath his robes.

Priest: COMBAT SKILL 16   ENDURANCE 23

If you win the combat, turn to **220**.

159

You eventually come to a halt at the base of a huge fir tree. You try to stand, but the pain in your legs and side is so great that you collapse and lose consciousness. It is a sleep that will spare you the pain of the Helghast blades, but it is also a sleep from which there is no awakening.

Your quest and your life end here.

160

'Forgive me my lord, I did not mean to startle you.' The man seems nervous, and the open hand that is extended towards you is shaking quite visibly.

With some caution you accept the gesture of friendship, and sit with the man at a tavern table. The place is deserted save for a couple of mice gnawing at a large chunk of cheese.

'Captain Kelman has instructed me to take you to the *Green Sceptre*, but only if I am sure that you are the Kai Lord they call Lone Wolf. Can you prove your identity?' You decide you must show your mastery of one of your Kai Disciplines.

If you wish to demonstrate your Kai Discipline of Healing, turn to **16**.

If you wish to demonstrate your Kai Discipline of Mindblast, turn to **133**.

If you wish to demonstrate your Kai Weaponskill, turn to **255**.

If you wish to demonstrate your Kai Discipline of Animal Kinship, turn to **203**.

If you wish to demonstrate your Kai Discipline of Mind Over Matter, turn to **48**.

If you do not possess any of the above Kai skills, or if you do not wish to demonstrate your skill, turn to **348**.

161

The shop appears to be empty. You wait and look at the merchandise for nearly five minutes, but still no one appears. You are about to leave when you notice a map hanging inside the door. It is a plan of the Port of Ragadorn. The Ragadorn stables and coach station is clearly marked near the east gate of the city. This is where land transport can be found to take you to Port Bax. You memorize the map route to the east gate and leave the shop. You run back to Axe Lane and turn east into Sage Street. At the end of this winding lane you arrive at the Ragadorn Bridge, the only connection between the east and west sides of the city. You push your way across the crowded bridge and run along the cobblestones of East Trade Lane.

Turn to **186**.

162

He bellows his battle-cry and lunges at your head.

Knight of the White Mountain:
COMBAT SKILL 20   ENDURANCE 27

You may evade combat at any time by running into the trees and turning to **244**.

If you win the combat, turn to **302**.

163

'We've a full sail and a sharp prow. There's not a warship on the northern seas that'll catch the Green Sceptre,' said the captain.

He is proved right, for the pirate ship soon disappears over the horizon. 'Twenty-five years at sea and I've never known the Lakuri pirates to venture this far north to raid,' he said, stroking his beard thoughtfully. 'They must be after a valuable cargo to sail so far from their tropical islands.'

As the captain descends below deck to his cabin, you get an uneasy feeling that the valuable cargo may be you.

Turn to **240**.

164

You have walked for nearly a mile along this deserted tunnel when you see a flight of steps cut into the rockface to your left. They lead to a platform which runs the length of the tunnel ceiling. It is used to service the torches.

If you wish to climb the steps and investigate the platform, turn to **52**.

If you wish to ignore the steps and continue on your journey, turn to **256**.

If you have the Kai Discipline of Sixth Sense, turn to **172**.

165

Placing the gold in your pouch, you remove the Seal and hand it to her. She snatches it and examines it closely. As you leave the shop, you hear her sniggering quietly to herself, and you wonder if you have done the right thing.

Turn to **186**.

166 – *Illustration X*

You make your way up a flight of stairs and on to the crowded deck. Fierce battle rages all around you as the Durenese fleet is engulfed by the rush of ghostly death-hulks. Suddenly a flash of searing flame shoots from a tower at the rear of the death-hulk you are on, and explodes into the side of a Durenese warship less than fifty yards away. You watch with horror as soldiers leap from the deck, their clothes and hair in flames.

If you wish to investigate the tower, turn to **328**.

If you wish to escape from this ship, jump overboard by turning to **267**.

X.   Soldiers leap from the deck, their clothes and hair in flames

167

'You play a daring strategy, Lone Wolf. But I think I have you now.'

Captain Kelman moves his ornate keystone across to your side of the board with a triumphant smile. But it soon fades to a look of shock as you unexpectedly counter his move. 'Stalemate,' you reply coolly. The captain stares at the board in disbelief.

'The skills of the Kai never cease to amaze me,' he says, slowly scratching his head. He is still staring at the Samor board when you finally bid him goodnight and return to your cabin.

Turn to **197**.

168

Slowly, one by one, the other travellers appear and stare in shock at the dead coachman. 'We must bury him,' says the priest.

You silently nod your agreement and prepare a grave in which to lay the corpse. As you all walk back to the coach, you discuss what should be done.

'I know the road to Port Bax. I had better drive the coach,' volunteers Halvorc.

'I do hope we're not blamed for his death,' says the priest nervously.

'It was an act of the gods,' says Dorier.

'I shall testify to that,' says Ganon. 'Lies are never spoken by Knights of the White Mountain.'

It is true that in Durenor, a true knight will speak only the truth whether for his own good or ill. His words seem to reassure the priest, and you are all soon once more on the road heading towards the eastern horizon. It is late in the afternoon when you arrive at a coach station in a small coastal village known as Gorn Cove, which is mainly populated by outcasts, thieves and Szalls.

The death of the coachman is met by the villagers, with great suspicion, but Dorier's words convince them that it was accidental.

There is only one inn at the village, a tavern known as the Forlorn Hope. Its state of disrepair is typical of all the other hovels in this poor sea village. A room for the night costs 1 Gold Crown.

If you can pay for the room, turn to **314**.
If you cannot, turn to **25**.

169

You leave the gaming house and walk dejectedly back towards the coach station. In the distance you can see the east gate of the city. Waiting below it is the coach to Durenor. You must get to Port Bax – the future of Sommerlund depends on it. You slip past the guard and board the coach without him seeing you enter. As the departure time gets nearer, five other passengers climb into the coach and seat themselves around you. The guard slams the door and you begin your journey to Port Bax.

Pick a number from the *Random Number Table*.

If the number you have picked is *0–3*, turn to **39**.
If the number is *4–6*, turn to **249**.
If the number is *7–9*, turn to **339**.

170

The guard looks at your white card and sneers, 'This is a merchant's pass. It's of no use to you here. You must have a red pass to gain access to the naval quadrant.' He flicks the card back at you and returns to his post at the gate.

Turn to **327**.

171

Behind the trees you notice a wide coast road running from east to west.

If you wish to head east, turn to **27**.
If you wish to head west, turn to **114**.

172

Your Kai sense warns you that there is something evil hiding in the darkness of the platform.

If you wish to climb the stone steps and confront it, turn to **52**.
If you wish to sprint past the steps and platform, turn to **256**.
If you want to run back to the junction and take the left path, turn to **64**.

173

You enter a magnificent emporium in which are displayed some of the finest goods of northern Magnamund. Even at this late hour, the trading post is busy, as captains and rich merchants haggle over the sale or exchange of their cargoes. The owner of the trading post appears to be a young warrior, who presides over the auction of goods from an ornate chair held up by four massive chains. His men are all dressed in black armour, and on their shields they bear the emblem of a black ship on a red crest.

Then, by chance, you notice a small boy steal a money pouch from the belt of a merchant, and slip it into his boot.

If you decide to grab the boy and make him hand back the pouch, turn to **91**.

If you follow the boy outside and steal the pouch from him, turn to **6**.

If you just ignore what you have seen, and examine the goods for sale, turn to **283**.

174

The knight steps towards you and says, 'I've yet to meet a peasant who could afford to buy his own horse. You are not a peasant, but I'd wager you to be a thief.'

With a flick of his broadsword, he unhorses you and heavily you fall to the ground. Instinctively, you draw your weapon in self-defence as the knight attacks you.

Turn to **162**.

175

'It seems our bird has flown,' says the captain, pointing to a longboat moving swiftly towards another ship on the horizon. 'She flies no flag, and her hull is of a strange shape. I've ne'er before seen the like.'

You watch as the longboat reaches the mysterious ship. As if by magic a sea fog appears from nowhere and engulfs the vessel. Moments later, both the ship and the fog have disappeared.

Pick a number from the *Random Number Table*.

If the number you have picked is *0–4*, turn to **53**.
If the number is *5–9*, turn to **209**.

176 – *Illustration XI*

For three days and nights, you have ridden along the highway as it follows its route up the river valley of the Durenon. In the distance are the peaks of the Hammerdal mountains, one of the highest ranges in all Magnamund. The capital lies at the very centre of those mountains.

It is now the morning of the fourteenth day of your quest. You have made camp near a waterfall where the fast-flowing Durenon drops over 120 feet. You are about to leave, when a group of six hooded riders appears on the forest highway above, blocking your exit from the camp.

XI.   Lord-lieutenant Rhygar demands that they let you pass
      as you bear a royal despatch

Lord-lieutenant Rhygar demands that they let you pass, adding that you bear a royal dispatch. In Durenor, it is a treasonable offence to hinder a king's messenger, but unfortunately, the cloaked riders do not seem impressed by his warning, and they remain where they are.

'If you do not care for reason, perhaps our swords will turn your tails,' says Rhygar. He draws his sword, and orders his men to attack.

If you wish to follow Rhygar, turn to **45**.

If you do not want to attack the riders, turn to **277**.

If you have the Kai Discipline of Sixth Sense, turn to **322**.

177

As you re-enter the tavern, you can see that most of the sailors are clustered around the centre table to watch an arm-wrestling contest.

If you wish to enter the contest, turn to **276**.

If you wish to talk with the innkeeper, turn to **342**.

178

Although the delicious smell of the food is making your mouth water, you suspect that something is very wrong. You set the tray down by the door. Your hunger has made you tired, and you decide to take a short nap before meeting the others in the bar.

When you awake, you see the bodies of two dead rats lying beside the food tray – they have been poisoned. The shock soon turns to anger when you realize that the poison was in the food intended for you.

You grab your equipment and leave the room, intent on discovering your would-be assassin.

Turn to **200**.

179

Using your Kai Discipline of Camouflage, you can hide undetected in the hay-cart until it is safe to come out.

If you wish to hide in the hay-wain, turn to **82**.
If you would rather take a horse and leave the village, turn to **150**.
If you wish to enter the wheelwright's shop, turn to **71**.

180

You conclude that the crew are either blind or have no intention of rescuing you. The fishing boat continues on its course out to sea and, without seeming to notice you, disappears over the horizon. Pulling off a loose plank from the hatch cover, and using it as a makeshift oar, you set about paddling towards the shore.

Turn to **337**.

181

This street seems dirtier and smellier than the one you have just been down. The cluttered window of a shop to your left catches your attention. In the window are many Useful Items, all of which bear a price tag.

Sword – 4 Gold Crowns
Dagger – 2 Gold Crowns

Short Sword – 3 Gold Crowns
Warhammer – 6 Gold Crowns
Spear – 5 Gold Crowns
Mace – 4 Gold Crowns
Fur Blanket – 3 Gold Crowns
Backpack – 1 Gold Crown

You may enter and purchase any of the above Items. Remember to mark them on your *Action Chart*. When you have completed your purchases, you continue your way along Sage Street, towards the Ragadorn Bridge. This bridge is the only connection between the east and west sides of the port and you push your way through the crowds of people and carts. You find yourself in a rubbish-strewn thoroughfare known as East Trade Lane.

Turn to **186**.

182

You must find shelter for the night or you will risk being arrested by the city guard. Your Kai sense tells you that the best course of action is to return to the tavern and ask the innkeeper for a room. Refreshed by a comfortable night's sleep, you can then make plans to reach Durenor first thing in the morning.

Turn to **177**.

183

The forest drops away steeply at the edge of your campsite, and in your haste you trip and fall headlong through the trees.

Pick a number from the *Random Number Table*.

If the number you have picked is *0–8*, turn to **311**.
If the number is *9*, turn to **159**.

184

As the Drakkar dies at your feet, the pirates falter at the sight of such a powerful warrior floored, and then flee to their sinking ship. Captain Kelman rallies his crew and leads them against the retreating enemy, driving them into the water with the fury of the attack.

The *Green Sceptre* pulls free of the pirate ship, which keels heavily to starboard.

'Our thanks, Kai lord.' The captain grasps your hand. 'We are proud and thankful to have you with us.' A cheer resounds along the deck, and the crew voice their praise.

You help tend the wounded whilst repairs are carried out to the damaged prow. Within the hour, the wind fills the sails and you are back on course for Durenor once more.

Turn to **240**.

185

As you race along the corpse-littered deck, two Drakkarim warriors emerge from a doorway and attack you by surprise. You must fight them one at a time.

Drakkar 1: COMBAT SKILL 17   ENDURANCE 25
Drakkar 2: COMBAT SKILL 16   ENDURANCE 26

You may evade at any stage of the combat by diving into the sea. Turn to **286**.

If you kill them both in combat, you can then jump to the deck of a nearby Durenese ship by turning to **120**.

186

You are standing opposite a large building with a sign on the wall:

RAGADORN STABLES AND COACH STATION

A green-clad coachman is sitting next to a notice board that reads, 'Port Bax – Journey Time – 7 Days'.

If you wish to approach the coachman and ask to buy a ticket for the journey to Port Bax, turn to **136**.

If you have no money, turn to **238**.

187

A quick search of their bodies reveals the following Items:

2 Spears
2 Swords
6 Gold Crowns

If you decide to take any of these, remember to mark them on your *Action Chart*.

You roll the bodies into the Rymerift and then run across the bridge in case anyone saw the incident. The forest track continues for over an hour before you arrive at a junction, where you see a signpost.

PORT BAX – 3 MILES

You adjust your equipment and set off towards the east.

Turn to **265**.

188

Your quick wits and skill have saved you from a venomous bite. As the snake disappears into the long grass beyond the road, you gather together your Backpack and climb the tree, where you spend the rest of the night safely above the ground.

Turn to **312**.

189

'Impostor!' he cries, and draws his weapon. Before you can react to his attack, his sword has grazed your arm and you lose 2 ENDURANCE points. He runs at you and knocks you backwards through the open doorway. In a tangle of limbs and curses, you both fall headlong down the watchtower stairs. You stagger to your feet, but the knight is already up and searching for his broadsword.

If you wish to fight him, turn to **162**.

If you would rather abandon your horse and run for the safety of the trees, turn to **244**.

190

Using the edge of a steel rule to prise open the lock, you suddenly feel a sharp pain in your chest. A cunning trap has been laid, and as you open the box, a small needle shoots out and embeds itself in your flesh. It is tipped with a deadly poison. You die instantly.

Your mission and your life come to a tragic end here.

191

At the end of the avenue, the cobbled street turns abruptly to the right. Opposite this point is a tall, white stone building with a plaque above the door.

You can see that the cobbled street ends at a high stone wall. There is a large red gate in this wall and it is guarded by two soldiers. Beyond the gate, you can make out the masts of ships moored in the harbour.

If you wish to enter the port watchtower, turn to **318**.

If you wish to approach the red gate, turn to **246**.

192

The drunken sailors roar with delight, money changes hands and bets are settled. You notice your opponent wink at two of his henchmen. They begin to move towards you. Without a moment's hesitation, you rise from the table and punch the sailor so hard in the face that he sommersaults backwards crashing into his surprised friends. You leave them sprawled in a heap on the floor.

As you reach the tavern door, an ugly sailor draws his sword and blocks your escape. But before you have a chance to do anything, there is a loud thud and he falls to his knees. Behind him stands the serving girl, a large wooden club in her hand, smiling at you. You thank her, and wink as you race out of the door and into the darkened street beyond.

After running blindly in the dark for many minutes, you notice a stable and coach station through the gloom ahead. With the shouts of angry sailors still ringing in your ears, you run to the building and climb a ladder where you spend the night safely hidden in the hay-loft.

Turn to **32**.

193

The voyage to Sommerlund is one of ill-omen. Deep black storm clouds gather on the horizon, and a fierce wind relentlessly torments the restless sea. At night, great bolts of lightning tear open the darkness, followed by a rolling thunder so loud that it shakes every timber of the flagship. Many of the soldiers aboard the fleet are mountain-dwellers, unaccustomed to the shift of the sea. By the third day, over half their number are so ill as to be unable to stand. Lord Axim is close to despair.

'How I pray that this storm will lift, for even if the fleet arrives intact, I fear our men will be too weak to break the enemy.'

Then, as if in answer to his prayer, the dawn of the next day heralds an end to the raging storms. But the calm waters now surrounding the fleet contain a danger far greater than any storm.

Turn to **100**.

194

When you awake, you are shocked to find yourself lying beneath a wooden jetty, and the shallow water surrounding you fills your nostrils with a foul stench. As you stand, your head throbs violently as if you had been knocked unconscious. This is exactly what has happened to you, and your Gold, your Backpack, your Weapons and *all* your Special Items (including the Seal of Hammerdal) have been stolen by the fishermen.

With a groan of despair, you climb out of the slimy water and pull yourself on to the jetty. Looking up you see a faded sign.

WELCOME TO RAGADORN

You fear the rumours about this place are true. It is nearly dark and it has started to rain. You must find the Seal if you are to persuade the Durenese to give you the Sommerswerd. Looking round, you see a large market square with a stone signpost in the centre, indicating the various roads that lead off the square.

If you wish to go east along Barnacle Street, turn to **215**.

If you wish to go south along Westbank Wharf, turn to **303**.

If you wish to go north along Booty Walk, turn to **129**.

If you would rather go west back to the jetty, and search for the fishing boat, turn to **86**.

195

You have been travelling for nearly two hours when the driver shouts, 'Toll bridge ahead. One Crown apiece.'

Looking out of the window, it is pouring down with rain but you can just make out a wooden bridge and a log cabin in the distance. The driver halts the coach at the log cabin and an ugly creature appears at the doorway. It is a warty-skinned Szall, a harmless and cowardly breed of Giak. They have been natives of the Wildlands since the Age of the Black Moon, when thousands of their kind migrated from the Durncrag mountains to avoid the tyranny of Vashna, the mightiest of the Darklords.

The Szall demands one Gold Crown from each passenger before the coach will be allowed to pass. The other passengers each place one Crown upon a small plate and hand it to you.

If you have enough gold to pay the toll, do so and
continue on your journey by turning to **249**.

If you have no money, turn to **50**.

196

King Alin IV sits alone in his domed tower, viewing his
mountain domain through one of the many portals of
tinted glass. You and Lord Axim are formally
announced as you enter the chamber, and you
respectfully bow to his Majesty. Then, Lord Axim
removes the Seal of Hammerdal from your finger
and walks over to the King's side. For nearly an hour
they talk, their sombre faces reflecting the seriousness
of the situation. There is a short pause of silent
meditation, and King Alin suddenly rises from his
throne and addresses you for the first time.

'Alas, the Darklords have woken once more, and
once more does Sommerlund come in search of our
aid. I had prayed that my reign would be
remembered as a time of peace and fulfilment, but
in my heart I knew it was to be otherwise.'

The King removes a golden key from the pocket of his
white robe and inserts it in a marble dais standing in
the centre of the chamber. A gentle humming fills the
room, as the stone cover slides back to reveal the hilt
of a golden sword.

'Take the sword, Lone Wolf. It is foretold that only a
true son of Sommerlund can release the powers that
lie within its blade.

As you grasp the glowing hilt, a tingling sensation
runs up your arm and radiates throughout your body.

If you have the Kai Discipline of Sixth Sense, turn to **79**.

If you do not possess this skill, turn to **123**.

197

As dawn breaks, a fierce storm rises and you are woken by the violent rocking of the ship. The floor of your cabin is awash, and the shouts of the crew can hardly be heard above the howling wind. You quickly dress, gather up your equipment and make your way to the deck.

You are soon joined by the captain, who takes hold of your arm and orders you to return to your cabin. Suddenly, as you start to go down, there is a thunderous crack as, high in the rigging, part of the mast snaps. You look up to see the shattered pole falling towards you.

Pick a number from the *Random Number Table*.

If the number you have picked is *1–4*, turn to **78**.
If the number is *5–9*, turn to **141**.
If the number is *0*, turn to **247**.

198

You have covered less than twenty yards when your horse rears up and bolts. You are thrown to the ground and you lose 1 ENDURANCE point. Brushing the dirt from your cloak, you curse as the animal disappears out of sight. You will have to continue your journey from here on foot.

Turn to **138**.

199

The innkeeper pockets the Crown and says in a mocking voice, 'You can get there by putting one foot in front of the other – like this,' and with a loud laugh he walks behind the counter and disappears into the kitchen beyond. You curse his trickery and leave the inn, pausing only, in your anger, to kick over his bucket of dirty water.

Turn to **143**.

200 – *Illustration XII*

By the time you reach the bar, the others are all seated at a large table awaiting your appearance. Drawing closer to the table, you realize you have found your would-be assassin. You will have to attack without giving any warning to your enemy, so study your fellow travellers carefully and then make your decision.

If you wish to attack the Knight of the White Mountain called Dorier, turn to **7**.

If you wish to attack the merchant called Halvorc, turn to **60**.

If you wish to attack the adventuress called Viveka, turn to **85**.

If you with to attack the priest called Parsion, turn to **158**.

If you wish to attack the Knight of the White Mountain called Ganon, turn to **270**.

201

As you rise, the snake hisses and strikes at your arm. You dodge to one side, but are you quick enough to avoid its deadly fangs?

Pick a number from the *Random Number Table* to find out.

If the number you have picked is 0–4, turn to **285**.
If the number is 5–9, turn to **70**.

202

The soldier salutes and allows you to pass through the red gate. You walk into an open square lit by the tall beacons lining the quayside. To your relief, you sight the marble pillars of the Sommerlund Consulate, and the familiar sun-flag of your country flying above it in the fresh night breeze.

As you climb the stone steps, you are recognized by the Sommlending guards on duty at the main door. They disappear inside and quickly return in the company of a tall grey-haired official. His anguished expression suddenly changes to a smile of joy as he beholds your ragged Kai cloak and tunic.

'Hope beyond hope! Thank the gods that you live,

XII.   The others are all seated at a large table awaiting your
        appearance

Kai Lord. The scant news that has reached us from the west has caused us great alarm.'

You are ushered inside and taken immediately to the envoy of Sommerlund, Lord-Lieutenant Rhygar.

Turn to **31**.

203

'Feeling hungry?' you say, peering at the two busy housemice in the far corner. 'Perhaps you would care for some cheese?'

Using your Kai Discipline, you order the two mice to bring the cheese to you. The sailor looks on in amazement as the two furry creatures deposit the cheese at your feet and then scurry away.

Turn to **268**.

204

The keen sight you have developed through your Kai Discipline of Tracking has enabled you to identify the talisman that sits on top of the black staff. It is the crescent and crystal star emblem of the magician's guild of Toran in northern Sommerlund. This man is a renegade of the guild and a traitor to your country.

If you wish to climb the tower and attack this treacherous magician, turn to **73**.

If you do not wish to risk your life against this powerful sorcerer, jump overboard by turning to **267**.

205

The innkeeper frowns at you and points to a side door. 'If you can't afford a room, you can go and sleep in the stable. '

As you walk towards the exit, you feel the stare of the other passengers burning into your back. The door is slammed shut and you stand shivering in the cold night air.

Turn to **213**.

206

You are woken during the night by the baying of wolves in the distance. Rather than risk being torn to pieces in your sleep, you climb the tree and spend the rest of the night in safety, high above the ground.

Turn to **312**.

207

You have walked less than a hundred yards when the track disappears over the edge of a precipice towards the deep waters of the Rymerift below. It is impossible to go on any further in this direction. You will have to return along the path and cross the river at the bridge.

Turn to **47**.

208

You have just passed the wagon when you hear a noise behind you. Spinning around, you scan the walls and ceiling but you can see nothing in the gloom of the tunnel.

Turn to **134**.

209

The crew start to whisper. You hear the words 'ghost-ship' and 'cursed voyage', but the muttering stops when the captain's voice booms out an order for all hands on deck. Only the creaking of the timbers can be heard as Captain Kelman climbs to the rear deck to address the crew.

'Men, we're three days' sail from Port Bax. The fire has robbed us of our provisions and our freshwater has been fouled. We shall have to steer a new course for Ragadorn, where we shall make good our repairs and replenish our stores. That is all.'

The crew seem pleased by the captain's announcement, and set about their duties with renewed vigour.

Then the captain turns to you. 'We're about eight hours from Ragadorn, my lord. My orders are to see you safely to Port Bax and pass you into the care of the Sommlending consul, Lord-Lieutenant Rhygar. But time is not our ally and I fear the repairs may take a week or more to complete. When we drop anchor, you will have to find your own route to Durenor – by sea with us or alone by the coast road.'

As you return to your cabin, the king's words haunt your thoughts: 'Forty days, Lone Wolf. We only have strength to stand against them for forty days.' You do not have long to complete your dangerous mission.

Turn to **197**.

210

You place both hands on your stomach and try to fight back the pain as you concentrate on focusing your skill. The familiar warmth of your healing power numbs the pain, but the poison is very strong and your struggle is not yet over.

Pick a number from the *Random Number Table*. May the luck of the gods steer your choice, for your life now hangs on the number that you pick.

If the number you have picked is *0–4*, turn to **275**.
If the number is *5–9*, turn to **330**.

211

'The consulate of Sommerlund?' he says in surprise, somewhat taken aback by your sudden appearance. Then, recovering himself, he says, 'Why, of course! It is in Alin Square, near the harbour. Turn right when you leave and right again at the end of the avenue. That will take you to the Red Gate. You'll need a red pass to enter, as the consulate is in the naval quadrant of the city. It's a restricted area.'

You ask the man how you can obtain a red pass.

'From the captain of the port watch,' he says. 'You're obviously a stranger to Port Bax; there are few indeed that do not know the answer to that question. The port watchtower is at the end of the avenue, just as you turn for the Red Gate.'

You thank the old man and leave the city hall.

Turn to **191**.

212

Unfortunately, you are without a weapon and he is an expert swordsman. The fight is desperate and short. He runs you through the body with a swift lunge, and as he kicks you from the roof of the wagon, you feel nothing. You are already dead.

Your life and your mission end here.

213

You climb to the top of a pile of sheaves of hay and pull your warm Kai cloak around your shoulders to keep out the chill wind. You quickly fall asleep, little knowing you will never open your eyes again. One of the other passengers on the coach who is an agent of the Darklords creeps out and assasinates you in the dark chill of the night. Do you know who it was?

Your life and your quest have come to a tragic end here.

214

Once you are inside, you are immediately aware that this is not a shop at all. The room is cold and bare except for a large table in the centre. You notice sinister large iron manacles attached to each of its corners.

You are in the headquarters of the Silent Brotherhood, Lachlan's notorious secret police. With a mounting feeling of terror, you remember the tale of another Kai Lord; of how he had been captured and accused of spying. He had escaped after being tortured for three days and nights. You are not to be so fortunate. The door has automatically locked and soon the Silent Brothers, who are at this moment observing you through peep-holes in the wall, will come for you.

It may interest you to know that after a long week in the prison of the chief inquisitor you did not let a single Kai secret pass your lips. It is a record that has yet to be equalled, but not one that spared your life.

Your life and your mission end here.

215

Thirty yards along on the left side of the street, you hear the sound of merriment drifting out of a large ramshackle building. There is a creaking sign above the door.

THE NORTH STAR TAVERN

If you want to enter the tavern, turn to **4**.

If you wish to continue along Barnacle Street, turn to **83**.

216

For three days and nights the mighty fleet of Durenor steers swiftly towards the Holmgulf, a strong wind filling the sails of the warships. But although the voyage is fast, the soldiers' confidence and eagerness for battle has slowly faded as if their will has been drained by some invisible vampire. Lord Axim is close to despair.

'This black mood that haunts our decks is the evil work of the Darklords. I know of their power to turn a man's mind, but the curse that befalls us is a sorcery we cannot even see to destroy. How I pray that this spell would end, for even if we arrive at our destination, I fear that we are too weak in mind to break our foe.'

As if in answer to his prayer, the black curse seems to be lifted from the fleet with the dawning of the next day. But the spell is replaced by a threat far deadlier.

Turn to **100**.

217

The big man looks at you and says in a cynical voice. 'The coach station. A coach leaves for Port Bax this afternoon. For a Gold Crown I'll tell you how to get there.'

If you wish to pay him, remember to mark it on your *Action Chart* and turn to **199**.

If you wish to leave the inn now, turn to **143**.

218

You look up from the dead captain to see the macabre faces of the other crew members. They are surrounding you. There are at least twenty of them and they are armed with cutlasses and axes.

You can fight them by turning to **43**.

Or you can attempt to evade by grabbing a nearby rope, and swinging across to the deck of a Durenese warship. Turn to **105**.

219

Already the venom is taking effect. Your wounded arm feels stiff and a cold sweat has broken out on your brow. Quickly you remove the Pendant that Banedon gave you at the Ruins of Raumas. Using a sharp point of the star, you cut a deep V through the two puncture holes made by the fangs, and suck out the venom.

The charm is lucky indeed – and so are you. You lose 3 ENDURANCE points but not your life. You decide to climb the tree and spend the rest of the night safely above the ground.

Turn to **312**.

220

Searching the body, you discover all you need to prove that he was the assassin. Inside his pockets, you find a half-empty vial of gnadurn sap, the deadly poison that was used to taint your food. Then there is a scroll written in Giak, giving details of your expected arrival in Port Bax. He must have located you at Ragadorn and hatched his murder plans there. You notice that the weapon he carries is a Darklord blade, fashioned of black steel and forged in the furnaces of Helgedad, the infernal city of the Darklords beyond the Durncrag range. Only there in all of vast Magnamund can black steel be made. But the final proof of his true identity is the serpent tattoo on his left wrist. The harbour thugs who attempted to kill you before you had even left Holmgard bore exactly the same mark.

His purse contains 23 Gold Crowns which you may keep. Do not forget to mark them on your *Action Chart*.

Turn to **33**.

221

The floor of the tavern is covered with the blood and bodies of the people you have killed. Outside in the main street, you can hear the chant of a mob. The local inhabitants believe that you are a mad murderer and they intend to lynch you. Quickly, you make your escape through the rear door as the sound of the mob gets closer.

Turn to **88**.

222 – *Illustration XIII*

After taking care to close his door, the captain opens the mysterious bundle and tips the contents on to his cabin table. A large charred earthenware jug and several blackened rags drop in a heap. They give off a strange oily smell.

'This was no accidental fire,' he says solemnly. 'This was an act of sabotage. The forward hold is a food store yet I find this oil jug and these soaked rags upon the floor. Someone on this ship is prepared to risk his life to stop us reaching Durenor.'

You both stare at the burnt rags as if they hold the answer to your questions. Suddenly a cry from up on deck breaks the silence.

'Ship Ahoy! Ship off the port bow!'

Grabbing his sword and telescope, the captain disappears through the door and up the ladder to the deck above.

If you wish to follow him, turn to **175**.
If you would rather make a quick search of his cabin, turn to **315**.

223

The guard stares at the magnificent ring in awe. The legend of the Seal of Hammerdal is well known to the

XIII.   Captain Kelman opens the mysterious bundle and a large
charred earthenware jug drops out

people of Durenor. It is said that of all the lost treasures of the Durenese, the Seal of Hammerdal is one that they would not wish returned. The guard's anxious face shows he clearly recognizes the ring's dreadful, significance.

'I will not hinder your urgent mission, but I cannot help you except to set you on the road for Port Bax. Continue on this forest path and you will come to a fork near a stunted oak tree. Take the left track – it is the quickest way.'

You thank the loyal guard, and push on once more into the forest. A mile or so along the road, you come to the fork and take the left track. It leads to a stone bridge across the Rymerift. The waters of the Rymerift are over one mile deep and up to two miles at its widest point. Near to the bridge you find a signpost.

PORT BAX – 3 MILES

You breathe a sigh of relief for you should arrive there in under an hour.

Turn to **265**.

224

The following morning you are woken by the cry of seagulls as they wheel and soar above the clipper. The wind is strong and it fills the sails. You breakfast with Captain Kelman who is in better spirits than the previous day. He tells you that the *Green Sceptre* is making good speed and should arrive at Port Bax, the main Durenese seaport, within a week. Suddenly you hear a cry from the crow's nest.

'Land off the port bow! Land a'port!'

You and the captain climb up on deck and brace yourselves against the fresh sea breeze.

'That's Mannon, the southernmost island of the Kirlundin chain,' says the captain, pointing towards the sharp rocky coastline in the distance. ' "Wreck Point" the traders call it. Many a ship has ended her days upon those granite teeth.'

Captain Kelman hands you an ornate telescope with which to take a closer look. The sharp rocks are festooned with the splintered skeletons of ships that have run aground, or were dashed against the shore in a storm. You stare in fascination at the shattered hulls, imagining the terrifying scenes of their destruction. Then, suddenly, high above the pinnacles of stone hovers a black shadow, like a small rain cloud. It seems to be moving towards you. Suddenly you realize what the 'cloud' really is. It is a swarm of large Zlanbeast and possibly some Kraan. The alarm is shouted along the deck: 'Prepare for battle!'

If you wish to stay on deck, ready your weapon and turn to **146**.
If you wish to return to your cabin, turn to **34**.

225

Seventy Durenese warships left Port Bax, but only fifty now enter the Holmgulf. The battle has claimed many brave men including Admiral Calfen, who died aboard the flagship *Durenor*, the first ship to be sunk. But despite the heavy loss, a great victory has been won, a victory which inspires the Durenese soldiers with new strength so that the past ordeal of both the voyage and the battle are now forgotten. As their optimism and determination return, all are eager to reach Holmgard and raise the siege.

It is dusk on the thirty-seventh day of your quest when you sight the spires of Holmgard on the horizon. The city still stands defiantly against the army of Darklords, although constantly under siege. Flickering in the darkness you can see the small fires which burn throughout the capital. A confident Lord Axim joins you at the prow.

'The moonless sky will aid us this night. We shall enter the harbour unseen. Come the dawn, my men will scatter the wretched foe like dead leaves upon the wind of a storm.'

As you enter Holmgard harbour at the head of the Durenese fleet, you unsheathe the Sommerswerd and prepare to fulfil your destiny.

Turn to **350**.

The innkeeper speaks with the gruff tone of a native Ragadornian. You discover from him that this seaport is ruled by Lachlan, son of Killean the Overlord who died three years ago of the dreadful Red Death plague. The innkeeper does not speak highly of Lachlan, whom he calls the 'Prince of Thieves'.

'He and his mercenaries bleed the people dry with heavy taxes, and if y'complain, you end up in the harbour with a dagger in your back.' The big man shakes his head and pours another round of ale for the drunken sailors.

If you wish to buy a room for the night, pay the innkeeper 2 Gold Crowns and turn to **56**.

If you wish to try your luck at winning some Gold Crowns at arm-wrestling, turn to **276**.

227

Marching along the centre of the street are four heavily armed city guards. Rather than risk being arrested, you quickly dodge into an alley on your left. The guards suddenly halt opposite the entrance. If one of them should turn his head, you will be spotted for sure. Behind you is a small window that leads into a crowded tavern. Without hesitation, you climb in as quickly as possible.

Turn to **4**.

228

They are Larnuma trees and their fruit is very nutritious as well as being sweet and juicy. After your Meal you feel much stronger. You pick enough fruit for 2 Meals and store it in your Backpack.

Looking behind the trees, you see a wide coast road that stretches into the distance to left and right. There are no signposts.

If you wish to go left, turn to **27**.

If you wish to go right, turn to **114**.

229

Your sense warns you that the wagon contains an evil presence.

If you wish to enter the wagon, turn to **134**.

If you want to dash past the wagon and run for safety, turn to **208**.

(contd over)

If you want to return to the junction and take the right hand tunnel, turn to **164**.

230

You follow the street until it turns abruptly eastwards into Beggar Lane. You can see how this street got its name, for there are scores of ragged men, women and children huddled in doorways, all holding out their begging bowls.

As you walk towards the junction at the end of the street, you are assailed from all sides with pleas for gold.

If you wish to give any of your gold to these beggars, turn to **93**.

If you wish to push them aside and continue on your way, turn to **137**.

231

The back door opens on to a small square, in the centre of which is a large tomb. The fishermen have disappeared into the gloomy streets; all that is except one who has slipped on the wet cobblestones and knocked himself out. He is lying in the gutter with his face submerged in a puddle.

You roll him over with your foot and search him. You discover 5 Gold Crowns, a Dagger, and to your great relief the Seal of Hammerdal on his finger. Mark on your *Action Chart* those items you take with you and continue.

If you wish to return to the tavern, turn to **177**.
If you wish to study the tomb, turn to **24**.
If you wish to head west along Tomb Street, turn to **253**.
If you wish to head east along Watchtower Street, turn to **319**.
If you have the Kai Discipline of Tracking, turn to **182**.

232

You are less than twenty yards from the tower when the guard steps forward and demands to know your business. You notice that the soldier is wearing the red coat of a Durenese man-at-arms, and realize that you have reached the border of Durenor. You need to find some way of getting past him.

If you decide to say you are a merchant on your way to Port Bax, turn to **250**.
If you decide to offer him a bribe, turn to **68**.
If you want to show him the Seal of Hammerdal (if you still have it), turn to **223**.
If you have the Kai Discipline of Sixth Sense, turn to **149**.

233

'We're bound for Ragadorn – due there by noon

today,' he says, his face almost completely hidden by the wide brim of his hat. 'A seat below will cost you 3 Crowns, but you can ride on the roof for only one.'

If you wish to ride inside the coach, pay the driver 3 Gold Crowns and turn to **37**.

If you would prefer to stay on the roof, pay him one Gold Crown and turn to **148**.

If you cannot pay the fare, you must leave the coach and walk. Turn to **292**.

234

Before you can defend yourself, the Helghast has smashed into you and you both fall on to the highway below.

It may be some comfort to learn that your death was swift and painless. Your neck was instantly broken and you were spared the agony of the Helghast's black fingers tearing and burning their way through your throat. The Seal of Hammerdal is now on its way to Holmgard, which will now fall to the Darklords.

Your life and your quest end here.

235

As you reach the landing of the next floor, you hear the door crash open and the angry mob pour through. At the top of the stairs, a Short Sword hangs on a hook by the fireplace. You may take this weapon if you wish. Looking around you, you see that there is only one way to escape from this room and that is to jump through the window to the street below.

If you wish to jump through the window, turn to **132**.

If you wish to stand and fight the mob as they run up the stairs, turn to **90**.

236

Suddenly panic strikes. The ship is thrown into a frenzy of activity as sailors grab buckets and blankets with which to fight the fire. Flames are roaring through the hatch cover, and it takes over an hour to contain the blaze. The damage to the ship is great. The entire store of food and fresh water has been destroyed and the mid-section of the ship badly weakened.

The captain appears from out of the smoking hold and approaches you, his face black with soot. He is carrying something in a bundle under his arm.

'We must talk in private my lord,' he says quietly.

Without replying, you turn and follow him to his cabin.

Turn to **222**.

237

The dead zombies lie around your feet. By now, the soldiers' fear of the undead has turned to sheer hatred. A chorus of Durenese battle-cries resounds along the deck. You lead the charge along a boarding plank and on to the deck of the death-hulk, cleaving the zombie crew aside like a scythe through wheat. Then suddenly a black-cloaked figure blocks your path, a twisted sword held in its shrunken black hand. It is a Helghast, and you must fight it to the death.

238

Helghast: COMBAT SKILL 23   ENDURANCE 30

It is an undead creature, so remember to double all ENDURANCE points that it loses as a result of your possessing the Sommerswerd. It is immune to Mindblast.

If you win the combat, turn to **309**.

238 – *Illustration XIV*

Opposite the coach station is a narrow street leading to a gaming-house with a sign outside.

NO WEAPONS ALLOWED INSIDE

You are excited by the chance of being able to win some gold and you quickly enter. Any Weapons you may have must be left with a guard at the door. You can recover your Weapons when you decide to leave. You are given a silver token worth 1 Gold Crown, that can only be used in this gaming-house.

The entrance hall opens out into a huge room where many gambling games are in progress. One that catches your eye is called 'Cartwheel'. At one end of a long table, an attractive young woman spins a black dish divided into ten sections marked 0–9. As the dish spins, she drops a small silver ball into it which eventually comes to rest in one of the numbered sections. Several merchants are seated around the table and they are betting heavily on the fall of the silver ball.

To play 'Cartwheel', you must first decide the number you would like to bet on and just how many Gold Crowns you would like to stake. Make a note of these numbers and then pick a number from the

XIV.   An attractive young woman spins a black dish divided into ten sections marked 0–9

Random Number Table. If you pick exactly the same number, you win 8 Gold Crowns for every 1 Gold Crown that you gamble. If the number you pick is immediately before or after the correct choice, you win 5 Gold Crowns for every 1 Gold Crown that you stake. There is a limit to how much you can win on this table: 40 Gold Crowns.

You may play as many rounds of 'Cartwheel' as you wish until either you lose all your Gold Crowns or you decide to pick up your winnings (maximum of 40 Gold Crowns).

If you have lost all your Gold Crowns, turn to **169**.

If you have winnings to collect, or if you wish to withdraw with what money you have left, leave the building and turn to **186**.

239

You try to apply your hands to the injured man's chest, but the Szalls are pulling at your cloak and trying to drag you away.

If you have the Kai Discipline of Camouflage, turn to **77**.

If you do not possess this skill, you must attack the Szalls in order to save the man's life. Turn to **28**.

240

After three uneventful days at sea, you find shipboard life rather dreary. If you have the Kai Discipline of Healing, any ENDURANCE points that you may have lost on your adventure so far are restored. This will bring your ENDURANCE points score back to your original one. If you do not possess the skill, restore half of any points you have lost in combat.

On the afternoon of the fourth day, you are talking with an injured sailor up on deck when you smell smoke seeping from the hold.

If you wish to enter the hold, turn to **29**.
If you wish to shout 'Fire!' turn to **236**.
If you wish to warn the captain, turn to **101**.

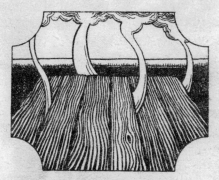

241

A hush descends on the tavern as the man you have accused turns to face you.

'You've got a careless tongue, stranger,' he says menacingly. 'It should be cut out before it does any more harm.' he draws a curved dagger and attacks you. The crowd form a circle around you both, preventing either of you from escaping. You must fight this man to the death.

Trickster: COMBAT SKILL 17   ENDURANCE 25

If you win the combat, turn to **21**.

242

Much of your time at Hammerdal is taken up by training with the Sommerswerd. Day by day your skill with the wondrous blade improves, and as you progress, so you learn more of its marvellous properties.

When you use the sword in combat, it will add 8 points to your COMBAT SKILL total (10 points if you possess the Kai Discipline of Weaponskill with any sword). It has the ability to absorb any magic used against you and doubles the total of all ENDURANCE points lost by undead enemies (eg Helghast) during combat.

You also come to realize that it is the only weapon in all of Magnamund that can kill a Darklord, and for this reason above all others they are determined to destroy you before you reach Durenor.

Turn to **152**.

Seeing their master slain, the Giaks falter and retreat towards the stern. Captain Kelman rallies his crew and attacks, leading his men against the snarling creatures and driving them back until they leap into the sea to avoid the rain of swords. Knowing the battle to be lost, the Kraan leave the masts and fly back to the distant coastline.

'Our thanks, Kai lord,' the captain says and shakes your hand. 'We are proud and thankful to have you with us.'

A cheer resounds along the deck as the crew voice their praise.

You help tend the wounded whilst repairs are carried out on the damaged masts. Within two hours they are complete, the wind fills the sails and you continue your voyage to Durenor.

Turn to **240**.

244

You push on through the dense forest for nearly three hours before you discover a track heading north, running parallel to the Rymerift, whose rushing waters are over one mile deep. In the distance, you spot a bridge that spans the dark water at a narrow point. A small hut with a flat roof has been erected in the centre, on top of which stand two soldiers. A sign points across the bridge.

PORT BAX

If you wish to cross the bridge, turn to **47**.

If you wish to avoid the bridge and continue along the path, turn to **207**.

If you have the Kai Discipline of Tracking, turn to **147**.

245

You turn east into Oxyoke Way and notice a sign above the door of a small shop to your left.

MEKI MAJENOR – ARMOURER AND WEAPONSMITH

If you wish to investigate the weaponsmithy, turn to **266**.

If you wish to continue walking east, turn to **310**.

246

One of the guards steps forward and demands to see your pass.

If you have a white pass, turn to **170**.
If you have a red pass, turn to **202**.
If you do not have a pass, you will be refused entry
to the harbour. Turn to **327**.

247

You are mesmerized by the falling mast and feel totally powerless to escape. As you are crushed beneath the enormous weight of splintering timber, the last thing that you remember are the horrified faces of Captain Kelman and his crew staring down at you.

Your life and your mission come to a tragic end here.

248

As you lay the golden sword upon the deck, the zombie captain dives at you and pins you down. His strength is unnatural. As he sinks a dagger into your throat, the last thing you hear is a hideous laugh of victory.

Your quest and your life end here.

249 – Illustration XV

During the course of the afternoon's journey, you chat with your fellow travellers and learn about their backgrounds.

Sitting opposite are two brothers named Ganon and Dorier. They are knights in the Order of the White Mountain, warrior lords of Durenor who have pledged allegiance to protect the country from raids by the bandits of the Wildlands. They own a castle and land near Port Bax. Next to them sits Halvorc the

1. Ganon
2. Dorier
3. Halvorc
4. Parsion
5. Viveka

XV.   You chat with your fellow travellers and learn about their backgrounds

merchant. His nose is swollen and his face is badly bruised thanks to Lachlan, the Overlord of Ragadorn. A little misunderstanding about port taxes lost him his cargo and most of his gold. Seated by the far door is a priest called Parsion. Like you, he is a Sommlending who has journeyed across the Wildlands by coach on his way to Port Bax. Beside you sits a young woman called Viveka. She is a mercenary adventuress who earns her gold by fighting for it, and sells her services to the highest bidder. She is returning to Port Bax having collected payment for a successful adventure in Ragadorn.

Not wishing to reveal your true identity, you have pretended to be a simple peasant. The travellers seem unaware of the war that now rages in Sommerlund.

Turn to **39**.

250

The soldier looks at you with a disbelieving stare.

'Where are your goods? Where is your horse or wagon? Merchants never travel to Port Bax on foot. You are no merchant – a bandit more like, desperate to put distance between yourself and some foul deed best left untold. Go back to where you have come from, scum. We have no need of the sort of goods you sell.'

If you are to get past this border guard alive, you will have to come up with an alternative plan.

If you wish to walk away, make a wide detour and enter the forest further south, turn to **244**.

If you want to try and bribe the guard, turn to **68**.
If you choose to reveal the Seal of Hammerdal (if you still possess it), turn to **223**.

251

It is nearly dark when the small fishing boat passes through the harbour entrance of Ragadorn. You have still seen no sign of survivors from the storm and you fear the worst.

You notice that three of the fishermen are acting very suspiciously. They whisper to each other and their eyes often glance at your money pouch. As the boat sails into the estuary of the River Dorn, they surround you and demand that you hand over all your gold. You are about to fight them when an unexpected blow from behind knocks you to the deck. You see one of the fishermen raise his foot. As it strikes your head, suddenly everything fades into darkness.

Turn to **194**.

252

You try to remember some of the stories told to you by an old Kai master called Wise Hawk. He was envoy to Port Bax for many years, and he knew and loved this city as well as any native Durenese. You recall him saying that the consulate overlooked Alin Square in the naval quadrant of the city. There is a sign to your left pointing along the avenue.

NAVAL QUADRANT – ½ MILE

Certain this is the right direction, you walk confidently along the tree-lined avenue.

Turn to **191**.

253

This street follows the harbour wall towards the River Dorn where it then turns south into Booty Walk. As you pass the warehouses lining the waterfront, you recognize the stone signpost in the centre of the square ahead.

If you wish to continue south, turn to **303**.
If you wish to walk along Barnacle Street, and return to the tavern, turn to **177**.

254

For three days and nights you have followed the highway to the capital as it runs parallel to the River Durenon. The river valley is a wide belt of rich, cultivated land that climbs towards the Hammerdal Mountains, one of the highest ranges in all of Magnamund.

It is on the morning of the fourteenth day of your quest, when six cloaked men appear at the edge of your camp. Lord-lieutenant Rhygar is the first to draw his sword. With a voice of authority he demands an explanation for their intrusion. In reply, they unsheathe black swords. Rhygar shouts to his men to prepare for combat as the cloaked strangers advance towards you.

If you wish to draw your weapon and prepare to fight, turn to **69**.
If you do not want to fight, you can evade by running into the woods before combat begins by turning to **183**.
If you have the Kai Discipline of Sixth Sense, turn to **344**.

255

Taking hold of your weapon, you demonstrate the Kai skills of balance and speed, as taught to you by your Kai masters. With breathtaking speed, as you spin and twist the weapon around your head and body, the movement of your hands becomes a dazzling blur. To finish your display of weaponskill, you strike the edge of a pewter plate and send it spinning across the room so fast that it embeds itself in the cellar door.

The sailor watches in amazement.

Turn to **268**.

256

You pass the stone steps and continue along the highway. You have just passed under the platform when you hear a noise above you. You stop and stare upwards but you can see nothing in the gloom of the tunnel ceiling.

Turn to **134**.

257

This rubbish-strewn cobbled street runs between rows of ramshackle, rot-infested houses and shops. The few inhabitants of Ragadorn that you see appear a cheerless lot, their faces haggard and drawn. They shuffle through the gloom, hunched against the pouring rain, their eyes fixed on the cobblestones at their feet. Then you reach a junction where Axe Lane bends towards the north and another street heads off towards the east.

If you wish to continue north and enter Black Knight Street, turn to **335**.

If you wish to head east, enter Sage Street by turning to **181**.

258

The stench of the ship is making you choke. You lose 1 ENDURANCE point. You must get out of this vile hold or you will suffocate.

If you wish to climb through the shattered deck, turn to **17**.

If you wish to leave the hold through a door in the far wall, turn to **5**.

If you have the Kai Discipline of Sixth Sense, turn to **272**.

259

Through the pouring rain, you can make out the dark shape of a city patrol marching towards you. Rather than risk being stopped and possibly arrested, you dash into a nearby shop.

Turn to **161**.

260

The captain orders the ship to go alongside and pick up the three men. They are fishermen from the Sommerlund port of Tyso. Their boat was attacked last night by pirates, and they are the only survivors.

You give them food and warm clothing and they can barely hold back their tears of gratitude. As you prepare to continue your journey to Durenor, one of the men offers you a fine Sword as a token of his thanks. If you wish to accept this gift, remember to mark it on your *Action Chart.*

Turn to **240**.

261

The road follows a course along a high, grassy ridge for many miles before turning northwards to the coast. You pass a village where the houses curve in a circle around a large pond of stagnant water. As you ride through, a gaggle of Szall children come running towards you, shouting and throwing stones.

You descend into the deep valley beyond and gradually the moor gives way to richer land that has been cleared and ploughed. The hillside opposite is heavily wooded. You are not far from the coast and you can see the tall cliffs with their multicoloured bands of rock jutting out into the ocean

Then just as you are passing through a small copse, you hear desperate cries for help off to your right.

If you wish to aid the person in trouble, turn to **95**.
If you wish to ignore their desperate pleas, continue riding along the road by turning to **198**.

262

The guard roughly pushes you aside and runs out of the watchtower towards Tomb Square. There is a small room off the staircase and you decide to enter and search it before he returns. In it you discover:

> Sword
> Mace
> Quarterstaff
> Enough Food for 1 Meal
> 6 Gold Crowns
> Potion of Orange Liquid

If you wish to take any of these items, mark them on your *Action Chart*.

As you are leaving, you collide with another guard and you both tumble down the stairs, but before he can gather his senses, you have sprinted off into the night.

Turn to **65**.

263

The man stares at the Seal with a look of shocked dismay. Without saying a word, he gets up from his chair and beckons you to follow him up a flight of spiral stairs that lead to a domed chamber. Here you meet the captain of the port watch. He listens intently as you tell of the war in Sommerlund and of your urgent mission.

'Issue a red pass immediately,' he orders. 'Top priority.'

You collect your pass, leave the port watchtower and hurry along the street towards the harbour guards.

Turn to **246**.

264

Focusing your powers of concentration on the snake's head, you will it to slither away in search of food. Slowly but surely your psychic suggestion works, and the snake eventually uncoils itself and vanishes into the long grass. Breathing a sigh of relief, you decide it would be safer to climb the tree and spend the rest of the night above the ground.

Turn to **312**.

265

At dusk on the tenth day of your quest, you experience your first sight of the magnificent city of Port Bax. Like a diamond set in the green velvet shore, the towers of the city glimmer in the pale light of a waxing moon. To the north is the harbour and the formidable warfleet of the Durenese navy. To the east, beyond the moss-covered city wall, stretches the forest of Durenor. And there, on the crest of a hill, stands a castle tall and proud, the crowning glory of this beautiful port.

You enter Port Bax through an unguarded gate in the green city wall, and make your way through the darkening streets towards the harbour.

As you turn into a tree-lined avenue, you notice the wide stone steps of a domed building to your right. You stop to read the brass plaque.

CITY HALL

Despite the late hour, the main doors are open.

If you wish to enter the city hall, turn to **84**.

(contd over)

If you wish to continue on your way towards the harbour, turn to **191**.

If you have the Kai Discipline of Tracking, turn to **252**.

266

As you enter, a bell rings and a small man in a padded leather jerkin bids you welcome. He is busy polishing a rusty suit of armour with a wire brush. The price of his weapons are displayed on a wooden board above the counter:

Swords	4 Gold Crowns each
Daggers	2 Gold Crowns each
Broadswords	7 Gold Crowns each
Short Swords	3 Gold Crowns each
Warhammers	6 Gold Crowns each
Spears	5 Gold Crowns each
Maces	4 Gold Crowns each
Axes	3 Gold Crowns each
Quarterstaffs	3 Gold Crowns each

You may purchase any of the above weapons if you have enough money to do so. The weaponsmith will also buy any Weapons that you may already have for 1 Gold Crown *less* than the price shown on his wooden board. Mark any necessary changes on your *Action Chart* before bidding him goodnight and returning to the street.

At the end of Oxyoke Way, on your right you find a large stable and coach station. It is now very dark and you must find somewhere to spend the night. Climbing a ladder at the side of the building, you spend a comfortable night hidden in the hay-loft.

Turn to **32**.

267

As you surface, you see that battle now rages all around you and the sea is choked with the bodies of the dead and drowning. You manage to swim thirty yards and scramble over the rail of a Durenese warship. Here, a bitter struggle is being waged against a long death-hulk that has grappled alongside. The zombies have clambered aboard and are slaughtering the terror-struck Durenese soldiers.

If you wish to draw the Sommerswerd and charge into battle, turn to **128**.

If you wish to jump on to the long death-hulk, turn to **309**.

268 – *Illustration XVI (overleaf)*

'You are indeed a Kai lord,' says the sailor, but the astonishment on his face quickly changes to an unpleasant sneer.

'Or should I say you *were!*'

As he speaks, a door crashes open behind you and you turn to see three harbour thugs advancing towards you. Each is armed with a scimitar and you have no choice but to fight all three as one enemy.

Harbour Thugs: COMBAT SKILL 16   ENDURANCE 25

You may evade after two rounds of combat by running through a side door. Turn to **125**.

If you win this combat, turn to **333**.

269

The horrific sight of the writhing creature fills you with loathing for the Darklords and their evil minions.

XVI. You turn to see three harbour thugs advancing towards you

When the Helghast has finally crumbled to nothing and you are quite sure that it has been destroyed, you remove the Magic Spear and wipe the tip on its smouldering robe.

Anxious to leave this place, you run down the tunnel as fast as you can.

Turn to **349**.

270

Ganon rolls away from his chair and draws his sword. An instant later his brother Dorier is by his side. You must fight them both as one enemy.

Ganon/Dorier: COMBAT SKILL 28   ENDURANCE 30

Due to the surprise of your attack, add 2 points to your COMBAT SKILL for the *first* round of combat only. Because of their exceptional strength of will, they are immune to Mindblast.

If you win this combat, turn to **33**.

271

You enter the tower archway and climb a stone stair where you are suddenly confronted by an armoured warrior. His head is encased in a steel helm and he wears the emblem of a black ship on a red crest. He steps forward and draws his sword saying, 'Halt and give the password!'

If you have the Kai Discipline of Camouflage, turn to **151**.

If you wish to attack him, turn to **157**.

If you wish to evade him by running from the tower, turn to **65**.

272

Someone or something is approaching the door of the hold from the other side. If you climb out through the shattered deck, you will leave your legs vulnerable to attack from below and there is no other way out. You sense that it is an evil creature of some considerable power. Raise the Sommerswerd and prepare for combat.

Turn to **5**.

273

You are about to strike when your assailant shouts, 'I am Ronan, my lord. I mean you no harm.'

You manage to divert your blow at the last moment, and your weapon smashes the back of a wooden chair. The beads of sweat that have broken out on the sailor's face appear to confirm that he speaks the truth.

Lower your weapon and turn to **160**.

274

A quick search of the bodies reveals a Sword, 6 Gold Crowns and a Mace. Take what you wish and mark them on your *Action Chart*.

Before you can leave by the front door, more angry villagers have forced their way into the shop. You can only leave now by the first floor window.

Turn to **132**.

275

You become weaker and weaker until your body finally surrenders to the welcoming arms of death.

Your assassin has successfully completed his mission.

Your adventure ends here.

276

A grim-looking sailor is challenging all-comers to an arm-wrestling contest. He is so confident of winning that he will pay 5 Gold Crowns to anyone who beats him. As you approach his table, a serving girl whispers in your ear, 'Be careful stranger, he is an evil man. He breaks the arms of those who lose, and murders any who beat him.'

As you face the sailor across the table, bets are made throughout the tavern.

If you have the Kai Discipline of Mindblast, turn to **14**.

If you do not have this skill, conduct the wrestling contest as if you were in combat. The first one to reach 0 ENDURANCE points, loses the match.

(contd over)

Sailor: COMBAT SKILL 18   ENDURANCE 25

If you lose, restore your ENDURANCE points to the
same total that you had before the contest, and
turn to **192**.

If you win the contest, turn to **305**.

277

As Rhygar and his men gallop nearer to the riders,
one of the cloaked horsemen draws a black staff from
beneath his robes. A fierce blue flame shoots from its
tip and explodes beneath Rhygar's horse, sending
him head over heels into the dense undergrowth.
Rhygar's men furiously attack with their swords.
Their sharp blades slice clean through their enemies'
cloaks and bodies, and then you realize that they are
having no effect. For these are Helghast, fell captains
of the Darklords. They have the ability to adopt
human form but they are invulnerable to normal
weapons. The cloaked staffbearer gives a hideous
laugh that tears at your mind. He is using a very
powerful Mindblast against you. You know you are
outnumbered by a superior enemy and you must act
quickly if you are to survive this ambush at all.

If you wish to abandon your horse and dive for
cover in the thick undergrowth, turn to **311**.

If you wish to aid Rhygar's men, turn to **59**.

278

You desperately wave your Kai cloak above your
head until you are near to exhaustion.

Pick a number from the *Random Number Table* to
see if your effort has been rewarded.

If the number you have picked is *0–6*, turn to **41**.
If the number is *7–9*, turn to **180**.

279

You recognize the creature to be a Noodnic, an intelligent but mischievous mountain-dwelling native of Durenor. The Noodnics inhabit a maze of smaller shafts and fissures that honeycomb the Hammerdal mountains, and live off whatever they can steal from the merchant caravans that travel the Tarnalin. It occurs to you that if you can catch the Noodnic, you may be able to learn if the Helghast are hiding within the tunnel.

If you wish to follow the Noodnic, turn to **23**.
If you would rather let it go and continue on your journey, turn to **340**.

280

You sleep deeply without being disturbed before rising at dawn, gathering your equipment and joining the others as they board the coach.

For two days and nights, the coach follows the trade route across the flat, treeless Wildlands. It stops only to allow the driver to sleep. But on the morning of the ninth day of your quest, there is an unfortunate accident.

Pick a number from the *Random Number Table*.

If the number you have picked is *0–4*, turn to **2**.
If the number is *5–9*, turn to **108**.

281

You beg the captain to pick up the unfortunate castaways but he ignores your pleas and orders the crew to continue with their duties. As the longboat disappears from view, you have a premonition that a similar fate awaits you. Shaken by the thought, you descend below decks and retire to your cabin.

Turn to **240**.

282

Both soldiers stab at you with their spears and try to force you off the bridge. As you lash out at one, the other dodges past you and attacks you from behind.

You cannot evade and you must fight them both to the death.

Bridge Guard 1: COMBAT SKILL 16   ENDURANCE 24
Bridge Guard 2: COMBAT SKILL 16   ENDURANCE 22

If you win this combat, turn to **187**.

283

You stare in awe at the variety of merchandise. Silk and spices from the opulent bazaars of Vassagonia; jewels from the mines of Bor; the finest weapons and armour from the smithies of Durenor; furs from the Brumalmarc of Kalte; cloth from Cloeasia; and all kinds of food and drink cover the tables.

Near the centre of the trading post you notice that the prices are displayed on large pieces of stretched vellum. One of the signs in particular catches your eye:

Swords	4 Gold Crowns each
Daggers	2 Gold Crowns each
Broadswords	6 Gold Crowns each
Spears	5 Gold Crowns each
Fine Foods	2 Gold Crowns per Meal
Gold Rings	8 Gold Crowns each
Fur Blankets	3 Gold Crowns each
Backpacks	1 Gold Crown each

If you have enough money, you may purchase any of the above Items. When you have concluded your purchases, you may leave the trading post by a side exit.

Turn to **245**.

284 – *Illustration XVII (overleaf)*

Cautiously, the soldiers surround you and take your Weapons and Backpack. The knight steps forward and raises the visor of his helm.

'Who are you? What is your purpose in Tarnalin?' he demands in a gruff voice.

You tell him that you are a Kai Lord from Sommerlund on an urgent mission to King Alin. He seems unconvinced by your words until you show him the Seal of Hammerdal. Then, without hesitation, he orders his men to return your belongings and ushers you through the wall of wagons. Beyond, you can see a horse-drawn carriage waiting in the centre of the crowded tunnel.

'Back to Hammerdal without delay,' he orders the driver, and you are thrown back in your seat as the coach moves off at breakneck speed.

You soon learn that the knight is Lord Axim of Ryme, commander of King Alin's personal bodyguard. He was on his way to Port Bax when the Helghast entered Tarnalin. He and ten soldiers were the only ones to survive a deadly encounter with these evil creatures.

During your ride through the Tarnalin, you must eat a Meal or lose 3 ENDURANCE points. The journey to the capital will take five hours and you are advised by Lord Axim to get some rest. As you slowly drift off to sleep, you begin a dream about the Sommerswerd. You picture a triumphant return to Holmgard and the defeat of the Darklord siege. Perhaps it will be a good omen of events to come?

Turn to **9**.

285

You feel the snake's fangs catch in the arm of your tunic, but that is all. You are lucky that the only damage done was to your clothing. As the serpent disappears into the long grass, you quickly climb the tree and spend the rest of the night safely above the ground.

Turn to **312**.

286

You hit the water and swim submerged for over a minute to avoid the falling bodies and burning debris of the battle. When you are finally forced to the surface for air, you catch a glimpse of a sight that raises your hopes of fulfilling your quest.

Turn to **109**.

XVII.   The knight is Lord Axim of Ryme, commander of King Alin's personal bodyguard

287

You focus your concentration on the small, brass lock. After a few seconds, you hear a faint click that tells you that the inner latch is now unlocked. Inside is a scroll bearing the royal seal of Sommerlund and containing confidential orders about your mission to Durenor. As you put the box back into its hiding place, you notice that a deadly trap had been hidden in the lid. Your Kai Discipline has saved you from the swift death of a poison needle. Closing the drawers, you quickly check that nothing looks as though it has been disturbed before joining the captain on deck.

Turn to **175**.

288

Without uttering a word, the knight points to the woods behind you and returns to the watchtower. He disappears inside and bolts the door.

The forest here is very thick and the undergrowth is a tangle of weeds and briars. It will be impossible to enter the wood on horseback. You realize you will have to abandon your mount and continue on foot.

Turn to **244**.

289

You are welcomed by an old woman dressed from head to toe in white. She smiles and offers you a delicious cup of Jala. Your experience of Ragadorn so far makes you suspicious of the dark liquid and you politely refuse her offer. As you push the steaming mug away, she notices the seal on your finger.

'What a magnificent ring! Is it for sale?' she asks, her eyes lighting up with excitement. You tell her firmly that it is not but she will not accept your refusal. She offers you any choice of the hundreds of potions that fill the glass cabinets behind her counter. As you turn to leave, she offers you 40 Gold Crowns.

If you wish to accept her offer, turn to **165**.
If you wish to leave the shop, turn to **186**.

290

The food smells delicious, but you notice that there are two or three drops of clear liquid on the side of the plate and another on the tray. At first you suspect that it is only water, until you touch the fluid and notice that it is sticky. You recognize it as sap from the gnadurn tree, a deadly poison used by assassins because of its lack of flavour or scent. The shock of your discovery soon turns to anger and you race out of the room, intent on discovering the identity of your enemy.

Turn to **200**.

291

The forest here is extremely dense and the under-growth is a tangle of bushy weeds. You ride for a mile in either direction and discover no track or path near the watchtower. If you are to reach Port Bax you must dismount and enter the forest on foot.

Turn to **244**.

292

You have been walking in the rain for over three hours when you are confronted by seven horsemen.

They are mercenaries employed by the Overlord of Ragadorn and they bear his emblem, a black ship on a red crest, upon their shields.

They demand that you hand over all your gold or they will kill you. When they discover that you have no gold, they chase you and eventually cut you down with their longswords. As you lie dying on the road, the last sight that you remember is the outline of Ragadorn on the distant horizon.

Your life and your quest come to a tragic end here.

293

This road eventually ends at a deserted forest cabin. Although it is furnished, a layer of fine dust covers everything inside and indicates that this place has not been used for several months. It is a dead end, and you have wasted precious time. You must return to the fork and take the left path without further delay.

Turn to **155**.

294

As you wrap the injured man in a large blanket, he drifts off into a sleep from which he will never awake. Back on deck, the bodies of the dead crew have been laid together.

Captain Kelman approaches and hands you a vicious-looking blade. 'This is no pirate sword, Lone Wolf. This weapon was forged in the furnaces of Helgedad. It is a Darklord blade.'

You cast the evil sword into the sea where it quickly sinks beneath the waves, and return to the *Green*

Sceptre. As the crew make ready to set sail for the east, you watch with sorrow as the Durenese trader sinks beneath the waves.

Turn to **240**.

295

A creature, much larger than the others and dressed in a magnificent robe of patchwork silk, screams an order in their strange language. All of the furry creatures arm themselves with spears and swords that look as if they have been crafted from broken wagon spokes and broom handles. With a strange battle-cry that sounds like 'Gashgiss – Nashgiss', they charge towards you. Your curiosity soon gives way to the realization that you must evade them or be trampled to death by the sheer weight of their numbers.

You turn and sprint along the narrow corridor until their angry cries begin to fade. You reach the entrance to where the passage connects with the main tunnel, and continue your journey from there.

Turn to **340**.

296

The people flee the tavern as the town guard attack. There are six of them and you must fight them one at a time.

Town Guard Sergeant:
COMBAT SKILL 13   ENDURANCE 22

Town Guard Corporal:
COMBAT SKILL 12   ENDURANCE 20

Town Guard 1:

(contd over)

COMBAT SKILL 11   ENDURANCE 19

Town Guard 2:

COMBAT SKILL 11   ENDURANCE 19

Town Guard 3:

COMBAT SKILL 10   ENDURANCE 18

Town Guard 4:

COMBAT SKILL 10   ENDURANCE 17

You may evade at any time by running out of the back door, and turning to **88**.

If you kill all of the town guard in combat, turn to **221**.

297

Halfway along this street on the left-hand side is a large stable and coach station. As it is now completely dark, you decide to enter. You spend the night safely hidden in the hay-loft of the stables.

Turn to **32**.

298

You hear the footsteps behind you quicken, and you spin round just in time to see them draw their daggers to attack you. If you do not have a Weapon, you must deduct 4 points from your COMBAT SKILL and fight them open-handed. They attack you one at a time.

Street Thief Leader:

COMBAT SKILL 15   ENDURANCE 23

Street Thief 1:

COMBAT SKILL 13   ENDURANCE 21

Street Thief 2:

COMBAT SKILL 13   ENDURANCE 20

You may evade the combat at any time by turning to **121**.

If you win the combat and kill all three street thieves, turn to **301**.

299

For six hours you run without rest. The Helghast are on the highway and you are forced to make your way through the steep and wooded foothills to avoid the risk of capture. Many times you feel that you just cannot go on, that the pain and the fatigue are too much to bear. But each time you falter, you are spurred on by Rhygar. You marvel at his endurance, for he is not a young man and he is clothed in the heavy armour of a Sommlending knight.

By nightfall, you have reached the entrance to Tarnalin, the western tunnel through the Hammerdal mountains. The three tunnels of Durenor were excavated during the age of the Black Moon, and each tunnel is over forty miles long and passes through the huge circle of the Hammerdal range to the capital. The tunnels provide the only access to the city.

Rhygar sits beside you and takes some bread and meat from his pack. 'Eat this, Lone Wolf. You must sustain your strength for the journey to Hammerdal, for from here you must venture alone through the Tarnalin. I shall remain here and hold the enemy back for as long as I have the strength to fight. Do not argue – that your mission should succeed is the only thing that matters.'

If Rhygar is to hold off the Helghast, he will need a

magic weapon as his own sword is of no use against the creatures.

> If you wish to give him your Magic Spear, so that he can defend the tunnel entrance, turn to **102**.
>
> If you do not possess a Magic Spear, or do not wish to give it to Rhygar, turn to **118**.

As you paddle towards the sleek trade caravel, you notice to your surprise that the boarding ladder is being pulled up. A mean-looking sailor leans over the gunwale and curses at you. He seems to think that you are a refugee trying to stowaway on board. But when you shout that you are Lone Wolf and you were ambushed by an impostor at the tavern, the ladder is soon lowered again. As you climb over the side of the ship, you are met by a tall man in a gold-braided uniform. His face is almost totally covered by a shock of bright red hair and a bright red beard.

'Haul anchor!' he booms. The crew spring into action as if their very lives depended on it.

The captain ushers you below to his cabin where he pours two glasses of Wanlo, a strong spirit. His face shows concern as you tell him what has happened.

'There is evil treachery at work and the enemy already has plans afoot to thwart your quest,' he begins when you've told your tale. 'It seems that you have lost the element of surprise – and I have lost a courageous first mate. Let us only hope that the voyage to Durenor be swift and safe.'

You leave him to go up on deck just in time to see the outline of Holmgard on the horizon. With mixed feelings of pride and apprehension, you descend the stairway to your cabin as the last spire of the capital disappears from view.

Pick a number from the *Random Number Table*.

If the number that you have picked is *0–1*, turn to **224**.
If the number is *2–3*, turn to **316**.
If the number is *4–5*, turn to **81**.
If the number is *6–7*, turn to **22**.
If the number is *8–9*, turn to **99**.

301

You search the bodies and discover 3 Gold Crowns, 3 Daggers and a Short Sword. If you wish to take any of these, mark them on your *Action Chart*.

Turn to **20**.

302

Stepping over the body, you climb the watchtower stairs and quickly search the living quarters. You find:

Mace
Broadsword
Quarterstaff
Healing Potion (restores 3 ENDURANCE points)
Enough Food for 3 Meals
Backpack
12 Gold Crowns

Take whatever Items you wish and quickly leave the watchtower in case someone discovers you.

You realize that the forest is very thick in this area and you will have to abandon your horse and continue on foot.

Turn to **244**.

303

Piles of rotting garbage litter this stretch of the waterfront, giving off such an evil smell that you are forced to cover your mouth and nose with your cloak. Ahead to your left, you notice the glow of torchlight

streaming from an open door. Above the door is a sign.

RAGADORN TRADING POST
MERCHANDISE BOUGHT AND SOLD

If you wish to enter the trading post, turn to **173**.
If you wish to continue on your way south, turn to **18**.

304

It may be of some consolation to learn that your death was mercifully swift. The Helghast's fingers tore and burnt their way through your throat within a few seconds. But now the Seal of Hammerdal is on its way to the Darklords' city of Helgedad.

Your life and your quest come to a tragic end here.

305

There is a shocked silence as you scoop up the 5 Gold Crowns from the table and turn to leave, but as you reach the tavern door, an ugly thug draws his sword and blocks your exit. Just as you are wondering what to do, there is a loud thud, and the man keels over on to the floor. Behind him, to your surprise stands the serving girl with a large wooden club in her hand. You thank her politely and race out of the door into the darkened street beyond.

After running for ten minutes in the dark, you spot a large stable and coach station through the gloom ahead. With the shouts of angry sailors still ringing in your ears, you quickly enter the building and spend the night safely hidden in the hay-loft.

Turn to **32**.

306

The soldier stabs at your chest with his spear, but you quickly sidestep and it merely grazes your arm. The guard is determined to fight but you do not want to have to kill him in combat, so you decide to try and knock him unconscious.

Fight the following combat as normal, but double all ENDURANCE points lost by the enemy. When his score reaches zero, you will have succeeded in knocking him out. All ENDURANCE points that you lose still count as wounds and are deducted from your current ENDURANCE points total.

Border Guard: COMBAT SKILL 16   ENDURANCE 24

If you successfully reduce his points to zero, turn to **35**.

307

The guards look angry and ready to attack. You will have to think of something quickly.

If you decide to offer them a bribe, turn to **57**.
If you decide to show them the Seal of Hammerdal (if you still have it), turn to **140**.
If you think it is safer to draw your weapon and attack, turn to **282**.

308

A sailor called Sprogg sits beside you and explains the rules of the game 'Portholes'. First he shows you two diamond-shaped dice made of red glass. Each dice has ten sides and they are numbered 0–9. Each player rolls both dice and adds the numbers together

(0 = zero). If anyone throws two 0's, they shout 'portholes' and automatically win.

Each player stakes 3 Gold Crowns per throw. There are two other players in the game and they all place their stake money into a hat before the dice are rolled.

Pick two numbers from the *Random Number Table* for *each* of the other two players, and note these scores down. Now pick two numbers from the *Random Number Table* for yourself. If your total is higher than the other players, you win 6 Gold Crowns. If either of the other players beat your score, you lose 3 Gold Crowns. You may leave the game at any time, but you must stop playing if you lose all your Crowns (bad luck!).

When you finally decide to leave, you may return to your cabin by turning to **197**.

309

As you advance along the deck, the hideous creatures turn and flee from the golden light of your sword. You notice something strange about this death-hulk, something familiar, but you are not quite sure what it is. Suddenly, a ghastly voice behind you cries out your name.

You raise the Sommerswerd and spin around to face the voice. The sight that confronts you fills your senses with a mortal terror.

Turn to **26**.

310

You soon reach the end of Oxyoke Way where it is crossed by another street running north to south. It is now so dark that you are unable to read the street signs. You must find shelter for the night. To your right you see a light above a sign.

RAGADORN STABLES AND COACH STATION

Under cover of the dark, you enter by a side entrance and spend the night safely hidden in the hay-loft.

Turn to **32**.

311

You come to rest face downwards in a tangle of thick bracken. The ringing of steel and the horrible cries of the Helghast echo through the trees around you. You are stunned and cannot move until a hand grabs your arm and pulls you upright. It is Rhygar. His face is bloodied and his armour is battered and charred.

'We must flee these demons, Lone Wolf. Strength and steel will not avail us here.'

You glimpse the silhouette of six Helghast on the forest road above. Their minds bent on the slaughter of Rhygar's men, they fail to see you both slip away under cover of the wooded hillside.

Turn to **299**.

312

Although you awake to a cold and rainswept dawn, the branches of the tree and your Kai cloak have kept you warm and dry during the night. Looking along the coast road, in the distance you can see a wagon heading towards you.

If you wish to get down from the tree and flag it down, turn to **117**.

If you wish to try to jump on to it as it passes beneath your branch, turn to **89**.

313

The gruesome death-cries of the Helghast finally fade and you risk stopping for a few seconds to catch your breath. You wince as you discover that the creature's fingers have burnt into your neck. The wounds are very sore and painful and you must lose 4 ENDURANCE points. Tearing the edge of your tunic, you make a bandage before continuing on your journey through the Tarnalin tunnel.

Turn to **349**.

314 – *Illustration XVIII (overleaf)*

The innkeeper is a thin old man with only one eye. He hands you a key and points to a balcony opposite. 'Number two, the red door,' he says.

The other travellers each pay their one Crown, collect a key and make their way across the crowded tavern floor towards the stairs.

'We must make plans for tomorrow.' says Dorier. The others all nod in agreement. 'I suggest we meet here in the bar in one hour to decide what to do.'

As you close the red door of your room, for some unknown reason you recall the words of Captain Kelman when you left Holmgard harbour: 'There is evil treachery at work when the enemy already has plans afoot to thwart your quest.'

An hour has nearly passed when your thoughts are disturbed by a knock at the door. It is the innkeeper and he is carrying a tray of hot food.

'With the compliments of one of your friends,' he says, and leaves before you can ask which one. The food smells most appetizing. You have not eaten today and now you must eat a Meal or lose 3 ENDURANCE points.

If you wish to eat the hot food put before you, turn to **36**.

If you do not want to eat this food, turn to **178**.

If you have the Kai Discipline of Hunting, turn to **290**.

315

Keeping one eye on the door, you quickly search the drawers of an ornate chart table. There does not appear to be anything unusual about the contents. You find mainly charts, island maps and navigational instruments. You are about to abandon this fruitless search when you notice a small lever hidden below the tabletop. You push it and a panel flips open to reveal a small wooden box with a brass lock.

If you wish to prise open the lock, turn to **190**.

If you wish to replace the box and join the captain on deck, before he suspects something is wrong, turn to **175**.

If you have the Kai Discipline of Mind Over Matter, turn to **287**.

316

The following morning you are woken by the cry of the ship's lookout high in the crow's nest: 'Ship ahoy! Ship off the starboard bow!'

You climb up on deck and brace yourself against the fresh sea breeze. On the horizon, you can see the

XVIII.   The innkeeper, a thin old man with only one eye, is
carrying a tray of hot food

wooded coastline of eastern Sommerlund, but in the middle distance is a merchant ship that looks badly damaged. It is low in the water and has only one mast remaining intact. It flies the flag of Durenor but the flag is upside down, a signal of distress.

Pick a number from the *Random Number Table*.

If the number you have picked is *0–4*, turn to **107**.
If the number is *5–9*, turn to **94**.

317

The shriek of the dying Szall is soon echoed by your own death-cry as two crossbow bolts embed themselves in your back.

Your mission and your life end here.

318

You are standing in a large, empty hall. Opposite are two doors, each with a brass sign above them.

If you wish to enter the door marked 'White Passes', turn to **75**.
If you wish to enter the door marked 'Red Passes', turn to **62**.
If you wish to leave and approach the guards at the end of the street, turn to **246**.

319

The street ends abruptly at a large stone watchtower.

If you wish to enter the watchtower, turn to **271**.
If you wish to return to the tavern, turn to **177**.

320

You search in his pack and are horrified to find that it contains a scroll of human skin upon which a message has been written in a strange runic script. The only word that you can make out is 'Kai'. You also find an evil-looking dagger with a black blade, and a block of cold obsidian.

These items bear the signs of the Darklords' craft. Something is very wrong here. You drop the pack as quickly as if it were red-hot and turn to mount your horse. To your dismay, you find it is no longer there: the Szalls must have stolen it. Wearily, you realize you will now have to continue your journey on foot.

Turn to **138**.

321

The meal is poor. It is made up of yesterday's leftovers, and what the captain tells you as you finish your meagre supper confirms your suspicions.

'I have a confession to make, Kai lord. The fire destroyed our entire food store; we had barely enough in the galley for this meal. I fear that we will have to survive on a diet of fresh fish until we reach Port Bax.'

Unless you have food in your Backpack, the poor meal leaves you hungry and you lose 2 ENDURANCE points.

After dinner, the captain challenges you to a game of Samor, a board game a little like chess, involving skilful strategy and bluff. To add a little excitement, he suggests a small wager.

If you wish to accept his offer, turn to **12**.

(contd over)

If you wish to decline the game, bid the captain goodnight and return to your cabin to sleep by turning to **197**.

322

There is a strong aura of evil surrounding these cloaked riders. Your Kai sense warns you not to follow Rhygar and his men on their impetuous charge. You shout a warning to them to stop them attacking, but it is too late. You cannot be heard above their battle-cries and the thundering hooves of their mounts.

Turn to **277**.

323

You follow this dingy street until it turns sharply eastwards into Lookout Street. In the far distance, you can see the River Dorn which separates the east and west sides of Ragadorn.

As you walk through the pouring rain, three suspicious men appear from an alley to start to follow you.

If you wish to stop and confront these men, turn to **131**.

If you wish to continue walking, turn to **298**.

If you would prefer to run towards the river, turn to **121**.

324

Will you:

Say you are lost and ask for shelter for the night? Turn to **135**.

Pretend to be a peasant looking for work? Turn to **174**.

Decide to ask directions for Port Bax? Turn to **288**.

325

You sense that the left tunnel is the quickest route to Hammerdal by about two miles. Just before you reach the junction you come across a large puddle in the centre of the highway. You notice that two sets of footprints, about the size and shape of a man's boot trail away from the water and lead off into both tunnels. The prints are still wet and you judge that they were made within the last twenty minutes.

If you wish to enter the left tunnel, turn to **64**.
If you wish to enter the right tunnel, turn to **164**.

326 – *Illustration XIX (overleaf)*

The captain orders the crew to hoist all the sails to attempt to outrun the vessel, but the pirate ship is fast and is trying to cross the bows of the *Green Sceptre*. A collision seems imminent.

'Prepare to ram,' the captain cries, as the side of the red-sailed warship looms up directly in front of the prow. There is an enormous crack of splintered timber as the *Green Sceptre* punches a large hole into the side of the pirate ship, and you are thrown to the deck with a jolt.

As the pirates clamber aboard, you are horrified to see the black-clad shape of a Drakkarim warrior in their midst. He has spotted you and he is advancing towards you, a large broadsword raised above his head. You must fight him to the death.

Drakkar: COMBAT SKILL 15   ENDURANCE 25

If you win the combat, turn to **184**.

327

You are slowly walking back along the cobbled street, trying to think of the best course of action, when a young boy approaches you. 'I can get you into the harbour, mister,' he says, 'but it'll cost you.'

He produces an envelope containing a sheaf of official-looking papers. 'These'll get you a red pass at the port watchtower. All yours for only 6 Gold Crowns.'

If you wish to buy the documents, pay the boy 6 Gold Crowns. If you refuse them, he will soon lose interest in you and will disappear. When you have made your decision, you return to the port watchtower.

If you wish to enter, turn to **318**.
If you would rather walk back along the tree-lined avenue to the city hall and enquire how you can reach the consulate of Sommerlund, turn to **84**.

328

Two zombies try to block your passage but you cleave them in half with one sweep of the Sommerswerd. You are at the foot of the tower and you can now see a hunchbacked man in crimson robes above you. He wears a tall, curved tokmor, a magician's head-dress. It bears the emblem of a serpent. In his right hand is a black staff.

XIX.　The black-clad shape of a Drakkarim warrior is advancing towards you, a large broadsword raised

If you possess a Crystal Star Pendant, turn to **113**.

If you have the Kai Discipline of Tracking, turn to **204**.

If you wish to climb the tower and attack the hunchback, turn to **73**.

If you wish to escape from this ship by jumping overboard, turn to **267**.

329

'Congratulations, Lone Wolf,' says the captain, as he wipes the sweat from his furrowed brow, 'you are a masterful player.'

He reaches into his waistcoat pocket and hands you a small pouch containing 10 Gold Crowns. You thank him for the game and offer him the chance to win back his stake the following evening. With a wry smile, he accepts your offer and bids you goodnight.

Return to your cabin by turning to **197**.

330

Within seconds, you are violently sick and then drift off into unconsciousness. It is nearly an hour before you awake. You feel dreadfully ill but you have survived the poison. Deduct 5 ENDURANCE points. As you slowly regain your strength, the shock of what has happened turns to anger. You grab your equipment and stagger out of the room, intent on discovering the identity of your would-be assassin.

Turn to **200**.

331

You quickly search the dead guard and discover a Sword, a Dagger and 3 Gold Crowns. You may take any of these Items and mark them on your *Action Chart*.

Suddenly you hear the sound of iron-shod boots descending the stone steps, and you look up to see another watchtower guard on the landing above. As you run into the street, you can hear him cursing you.

Turn to **65**.

332

You are in combat with a Helghast.

Helghast: COMBAT SKILL 21   ENDURANCE 30

It is attacking you with a powerful Mindblast. If you do not have the Kai Discipline of Mindshield, you will lose 2 ENDURANCE points for *every* round of combat that you fight it.

If you win the combat, turn to **92**.
You may evade at any stage of the fight by diving into the forest, and turning to **183**.

333

The sailor who claimed to be First Mate Ronan seems to have escaped during the fight. You quickly search the bodies of the harbour thugs, but find nothing of value. However, you do notice that each of them has a tattoo of a serpent on their left wrist. Whoever sent them to kill you must already know of the importance of your quest.

You leave the tavern by the side door and discover the dead body of a sailor lying beneath some stairs. Inside the collar of his blood-stained jacket is a tag bearing the name 'Ronan'. This must be the real Ronan. He has been murdered. You cover the body and turn towards the quay, where the *Green Sceptre* is anchored about three hundred yards from the harbour wall.

If you wish to use one of the many small boats or coracles that are roped to the quayside, turn to **300**.

If you wish to hunt down the impostor who pretended to be Ronan, turn to **67**.

334

After a few miles, the track becomes tangled and overgrown, until all trace of it has completely disappeared. The ride becomes slow and difficult as you strain to avoid the bogs and pot-holes of this moor.

After several hours you reach the edge of Durenor forest, and above the ferns, you notice a tall watchtower. A spiral of smoke rises lazily from a hidden chimney.

If you wish to enter the forest and investigate the tower, turn to **115**.

If you wish to ignore the tower and search for a forest track, turn to **291**.

If you have the Kai Discipline of Tracking, turn to **98**.

335

You notice a sign hanging outside a small shop.

If you wish to enter this shop and ask how you can reach Durenor, turn to **161**.

If you wish to ignore this shop and continue, turn to **61**.

336

In a fraction of a second, the searing burst of flame changes direction in mid-air and is drawn towards the blade of the Sommerswerd. The bolt of energy disappears into the golden blade like water into a drain. (You remember that the Sommerswerd has the power to absorb magic. This power has saved you from certain death.)

The sorcerer curses you, pulls a jewel from his ornate tokmor and throws it at your feet. There is a flash of flame and a cloud of choking green gas billows up in your face, filling your nostrils with its acidic smell. You are forced to jump to the deck below to avoid the poisonous gas, and you just catch a glimpse of the sorcerer as he frantically paddles a small boat away from the death-hulk flagship.

If you wish to dive into the sea and swim after him, turn to **109**.

If you wish to fight your way back to a Durenese warship, turn to **185**.

337

When you are only fifty yards offshore, you slip into the waves and swim towards land. When you finally reach the beach, you sink your fingers deep into the wet sand and slowly claw your way up the beach to the shelter of some dunes. You are exhausted and very hungry. The only possessions that you have saved are your Gold Crowns, your Backpack and any Special Items that you did not discard in the storm. Any weapons that you possessed before the storm have been lost. Make the necessary adjustment to your *Action Chart*. However, a few hundred yards away, you notice clumps of small twisted trees laden with purple fruit.

If you wish to eat this fruit, turn to **228**.

If you do not wish to eat this fruit, lose 3 ENDURANCE points and turn to **171**.

If you have the Kai Discipline of Hunting, turn to **139**.

338

You grasp the haft of the spear and level it at the approaching Helghast. It shrieks a desperate cry for it knows that it cannot avoid being impaled on the sharp tip of your spear. The shock of impact knocks you backwards and you crash to the highway below, losing 2 ENDURANCE points. The Helghast hits the ground barely seconds later, driving the spear through its black heart, and dying instantly.

If you wish to remove the spear, turn to **269**.

If you would rather leave the spear where it is and run away from here as quickly as possible, turn to **349**.

339

After only half an hour, the coach is stopped by some armed horsemen. They wear the black ship and red crest emblem of Lachlan the Overlord of Ragadorn. They demand gold in payment for what they call 'exit taxes': one Crown from each passenger. The other travellers each place a Crown on a small plate and hand it to you.

If you can pay the tax, do so and the coach will be allowed to go on its way. Turn to **249**.

If you have no money, turn to **50**.

340

You have been walking along the deserted tunnel for a further half-hour when the highway splits in two.

If you wish to enter the left tunnel, turn to **64**.

If you wish to enter the right tunnel, turn to **164**.

341

Shattered beams and torn sails are all that remain of the unfortunate merchant ship. You ask the captain to search for survivors but he ignores your plea and orders the crew to continue their duties. As the wreckage gradually disappears from view, the nagging fear that a similar fate could await you makes your throat dry. You descend below deck and take care to lock the cabin door behind you.

Turn to **240**.

342

He is a mountain of a man, completely bald and with large gold rings hanging from each ear. He looks at you suspiciously and says, 'Ale is one Gold Crown, a bed for the night is two. Which do you want?'

If you wish to buy some ale, pay the innkeeper 1 Gold Crown and turn to **72**.

If you wish to stay here for the night, pay the man 2 Gold Crowns and turn to **56**.

If you want neither, but merely wish to ask him a little bit about Ragadorn, turn to **226**.

343

You sense that you were the intended victim of this supposed accident. One of the passengers is trying to kill you!

Turn to **168**.

344

Your Kai sense reveals to you that the strangers are Helghast, fell captains of the Darklords. They have been sent from the Darklord city of Helgedad on a mission of assassination. They have the ability to take on the appearance of humans and they are immune to normal weapons and Mindblast.

You turn to shout a warning to Rhygar as you run for the safety of the forest.

Turn to **183**.

345

A fierce battle now rages throughout the ship as the evil Giaks fight to win control of the *Green Sceptre*. Perched high up in the masts, the Kraan are rending the sails with their talons and razor-sharp teeth whilst the Zlanbeast have flown back towards Wreck Point to pick up more nets of malicious Giaks.

Through the body-strewn decks, a menacing shape looms. Both Giaks and sailors are cut down by the creature as it advances towards you. It is a Drakkar, a cruel warrior of the Darklords. Raising his jet black broadsword, he attacks and you must fight him to the death.

Drakkar: COMBAT SKILL 16   ENDURANCE 24

If you win this combat, turn to **243**.

346

The driver nods and hands back the ticket. The inn is warm but poorly furnished. You must eat a Meal here which will cost you 1 Gold Crown unless you have a Meal in your Backpack.

The Kai Discipline of Hunting cannot be used on your journey through the Wildlands, as it is a barren waste-land inhabited only by creatures called Szalls, a weak and cowardly breed of Giak.

If you can afford the 1 Gold Crown for the room, turn to **280**.

If you have no money, turn to **205**.

347

At the end of this street is a large stable. To your right, you can see some of the mob searching the shops and houses. Suddenly, one of them sees you and raises the alarm. 'There he is – there's the murderer!'

There is no time to think. You rush into the stable and freeing one of the horses you leap on its back. As you ride out into the moonlight, an axe flies through the air and grazes your shoulder. You lose 1 ENDURANCE point and make your escape into the night.

Turn to **150**.

348

The sailor's face changes from a smile to a sneer at your reply. He quickly moves away from the table.

'Perhaps neither you nor I are all we claim to be. No matter. You will not live long enough to discover who I really am!' You hear a door crash open behind you. Spinning round, you see three harbour thugs moving towards you. Each is armed with a scimitar and you must fight them as one enemy.

Harbour Thugs: COMBAT SKILL 16   ENDURANCE 25

You may evade after two rounds of combat by using a side door, and turning to **125**.

If you win the combat, turn to **333**.

349

You have covered nearly three miles when you see a group of wagons in the distance. They have been strung out across the highway to form a barricade. Soldiers in red uniforms line the roofs of the wagons and a large crowd of people have gathered behind them. You can hear their excited chatter echoing along the tunnel. As you get closer, there is a sudden silence as all eyes turn to stare at you. A detachment of ten soldiers, led by a knight whose shield bears the royal arms of Durenor, advances towards you.

If you wish to attack these soldiers, turn to **87**.
If you wish to raise your hands and walk towards them, turn to **284**.

350 – *Illustration XX (overleaf)*

Holmgard has suffered much since your departure. Many of the shops and houses you remember passing on your way to the quay, are little more now than heaps of ashes. The Darklords' army with their evil engines of war surround the walls, and the flaming arcs of fireballs shooting through the air, continually light the night sky as they rain down on the streets below. The people fight the fire as best they can, but they are hungry and exhausted and close to surrender. At first, as it enters the harbour, the fleet is mistaken for the enemy and cries of despair can be heard all along the quay. But as the first of the soldiers set foot in the city and unfurl the royal arms of Durenor, the news of your return spreads quickly. The cries of despair have changed to a chorus of cheers: 'The Kai Lord has returned.'

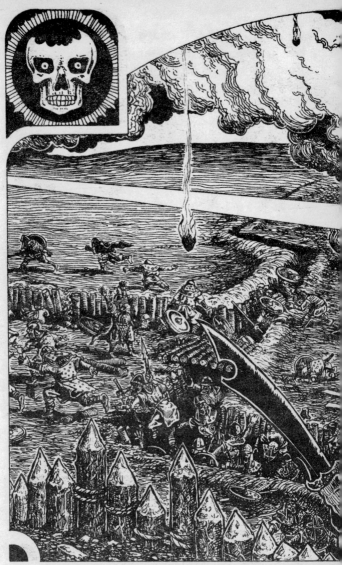

XX.   There is a mighty roar as the power of the sun-sword is
      unleashed in a searing white beam

You are standing at the top of the great watchtower, high above the main gate of the city, when the first light of dawn creeps slowly over the horizon. Thousand upon thousand of the black-clad enemy are massed around the city wall, huddled like beetles in the trenches that cover the plain. In the midst of this horde, a great red tent has been erected bearing the symbol of a broken skull. It is the mark of Zagarna, Lord of Kaag, a Darklord of Helgedad. His great ambition is the destruction of Holmgard; his fiercest desire to lead his army to victory over the House of Ulnar and claim Sommerlund for his own.

But victory is not to be his this day. Raising the Sommerswerd high above your head, a shaft of dawn sunlight catches upon the tip of the golden sword and a brilliant flash of blinding white flame runs the entire length of the blade. The power of the Sommerswerd electrifies you. Your senses reel and now your body reacts instinctively. You lower the Sommerswerd and point the blade towards the tent of Lord Zagarna. There is a mighty roar as the power of the sun-sword is unleashed in a searing white beam. The tent explodes and a brilliant fireball of white flame mushrooms skyward. A long and terrible cry rends the air. It is Lord Zagarna. The leader of the evil army is no more.

Gripped with fear and panic, the vast black army rise up and run in chaos from the city wall. The impossible has happened, their invincible master is slain. Again the Sommerswerd has returned to defeat them. The army and the allies of Durenor ride out of the city gates in pursuit of the panic-stricken enemy as they run blindly towards the Durncrag mountains. The victory is yours. Holmgard is saved and the murder of the Kai has finally been avenged.

But for you, Lone Wolf, a life of high adventure has only just begun. A new challenge awaits you and the Sommerswerd in Book Three of the LONE WOLF series:

THE CAVERNS OF KALTE

THE LONE WOLF CLUB

The Lone Wolf Club offers you exciting opportunities to become further involved in Lone Wolf activities. Joe Dever and Gary Chalk will be writing a newsletter for the Club and there will be competitions, events and the opportunity to collect Lone Wolf souvenirs.

If you are interested in becoming a member of the Lone Wolf Club, please write to The Lone Wolf Club, Sparrow Books, 17—21 Conway Street, London W1P 6JD, enclosing a large stamped addressed envelope.

CITADEL MINIATURES

A unique range of Lone Wolf models, especially designed by Gary Chalk and Joe Dever, are now available from Citadel Miniatures from around 40p. For details of these and Citadel's extensive range of over 1000 other models, please send a stamped addressed envelope to Citadel Miniatures, 10 Victoria Street, Newark, Notts.

Citadel miniatures are made especially for gamers and collectors. They are lead models and therefore not for use by young children.

LONE WOLF SOFTWARE

Fully interactive software adventure games for Lone Wolf 1 & 2 will be available in *September 1984*, for owners of the Sinclair ZX Spectrum 48K. A special feature of the program is a training sequence at the start of the game, in which the player fights with one of his teachers to set his COMBAT SKILLS for the Lone Wolf adventures.

Lone Wolf software will be available in bookshops and computer stores as a book-plus-cassette package. The cassette-only version can be ordered directly from the publishers at £5.95 each (includes VAT, postage and packing).

Send your order and cheque/postal order, made payable to the Hutchinson Publishing Group, to: Hutchinson Computer Publishing Ltd, 17–21 Conway Street, London W1P 6JD.
State clearly which program you require and allow 14 days for delivery.

RANDOM NUMBER TABLE

7	5	0	1	5	1	5	7	3	6
3	6	4	3	9	3	9	2	8	1
4	5	1	4	2	6	1	0	7	3
0	1	7	2	5	0	2	8	9	2
6	2	4	8	1	5	9	6	4	8
9	0	1	7	9	0	3	1	3	9
7	4	9	7	8	5	8	2	5	1
0	5	4	6	7	7	0	4	8	6
9	6	0	2	4	4	6	8	3	2
2	8	5	6	3	8	3	7	0	9